READING FOR THE CONTEMPORARY GUITARIST

Volume 2

IAN ROBBINS

©2020 Ian Robbins

All rights reserved. No part of this book may be reprinted or reproduced or utilized in any form or by any electronic, mechanical, or other means, now known or hereafter therein, including photocopying and recording, or in any information storage or retrieval system, without permission in writing from the publisher.

Trademark notice: Product or corporate names may be trademarks or registered trademarks, and are used only for identification and explanation without intent to infringe.

Library of Congress Cataloging-in-Publication Data
Name: Robbins, Ian Matthew, author.
Title: Reading for the Contemporary Guitarist Volume 2/ Ian Robbins
Identifiers: LCCN 18501751441 | ISBN 9781732996823 (paperback) | ISBN 9781732996830

ISBN: 9781732996823 (paperback)
ISBN: 9781732996830 (ebook)

Table of Contents

INTRODUCTION: 1

CHAPTER 1: READING IN TWO POSITIONS, READING HORIZONTALLY 2

MULTI POSITION READING: 2
HORIZONTAL READING: 7
    NOTES ON THE 1ST STRING 7
    NOTES ON THE 6TH STRING 10
    NOTES ON THE 5TH STRING 12
    NOTES ON THE 4TH STRING 14
    NOTES ON THE 3RD STRING 16
    NOTES ON THE 2ND STRING 17
ASSIGNMENT: 21

CHAPTER 2: INTRODUCTION TO POSITION VI, SIXTEENTH NOTE SYNCOPATION, AND PALM MUTES ... 23

SIXTEENTH NOTE SYNCOPATION 27
READING ARTICULATIONS: PALM MUTES 35
ASSIGNMENT: 37

CHAPTER 3: POSITION VI AND SIXTEENTH NOTE SYNCOPATION CONTINUED,   LET RING 39

SIXTEENTH NOTE SYNCOPATION CONTINUED 45
SIXTEENTH NOTE SYNCOPATION IN 6/8 TIME 49
READING ARTICULATIONS: LET RING 53
ASSIGNMENT: 54

CHAPTER 4: POSITION VI, HORIZONTAL READING AND SIXTEENTH NOTE FUNK ARTICULATIONS 57

HORIZONTAL READING 63
SIXTEENTH NOTE FUNK ARTICULATIONS 66
ASSIGNMENT: 71

CHAPTER 5: INTRODUCTION TO POSITION VII, SIXTEENTH NOTE SYNCOPATION WITH RESTS, AND COUNTERPOINT READING IN POSITION 1 73

SIXTEENTH NOTE REST SYNCOPATION 83
COUNTERPOINT IN POSITION I 86
ASSIGNMENT: 89

CHAPTER 6: POSITION VII CONTINUED, TIED SIXTEENTH NOTE SYNCOPATION, AND COUNTERPOINT READING IN POSITION I CONTINUED 91

Sixteenth Note Rest and Tie Syncopation 95
16th Note Reading in 6/8 98
Counterpoint Reading Continued 101
Assignment: 103

CHAPTER 7: POSITION VII CONTINUED, COUNTERPOINT READING IN POSITION II, AND BENDS 105

Temporary Modulation 107
Counterpoint Reading in Position II 110
Reading Articulations: Bends 112
Assignment: 117

CHAPTER 8: INTRODUCTION TO POSITION VII 8VA, SIXTEENTH NOTE SYNCOPATION WITH RESTS CONTINUED, AND COUNTERPOINT READING IN POSITIONS I AND II 119

Sixteenth Note Rest Syncopation Continued 127
Counterpoint in Positions I and II Combined 131
Assignment: 133

CHAPTER 9: POSITION VII 8VA CONTINUED, DOUBLE STOP BENDS, AND TRIPLE STOPS IN POSITIONS I AND V 135

Double Stop Bends 140
Triple Stop Reading 142
Assignment: 145

CHAPTER 10: POSITION VII 8VA CONTINUED, POSITIONS V, VI AND VII COMBINED, TRIPLE STOP READING IN POSITIONS I AND II COMBINED, ARTICULATION REVIEW 147

Combining Positions V, VI and VII 149
Triple Stop Reading in Positions I and II 152
Reading Articulations: Palm Mutes, Let Rings, Bends, and Double Stop Bends 154
Practice Charts: 155

ABOUT THE AUTHOR 158

Introduction:

Welcome to Vol. 2 of Reading for the Contemporary Guitarist. This book will pick up where Vol. 1 left off as you will begin to read in higher positions on the guitar neck. We will delve into rhythmic syncopation at the 16th note level and continue with more guitar-oriented articulations; such as palm mutes, let rings, and bends. You will be introduced to the concept of reading two melodic lines as once, known as *counterpoint* and develop strategies for connecting positions as you read. A very important concept for the professional guitarist is reading up an octave, or *8va* and this will be examined in this text as well.

The book begins with some review exercises in position connection. If any of these exercises seem beyond your level, it is recommended to go back to *Reading for the Contemporary Guitarist Vol. 1* and make sure you absorb all of that information. Everything here is designed to build off the last text, so without a solid foundation it will be difficult to master the concepts presented here.

Remember to practice reading daily. Work on both prepared pieces (assignments) and sight-reading (reading something fresh). Both are keys to developing not only your reading ability, but also your understanding of the guitar neck.

Chapter 1: Reading in Two Positions, Reading Horizontally

We will begin by reading in two positions. All examples will contain positions you are expected to be proficient in up to this point (Positions I-V):

Multi Position Reading:

Horizontal Reading:

A great way to improve position connection is to practice reading up and down on a single string. It is important to memorize all the note names on each of the six guitar strings as well as their visual position on the staff. Many guitar players are most familiar with the 6th, 5th and 1st string note names, as many roots of common chords and scales are found off the lowest two guitar strings, with the 1st string being a duplicate of the 6th string. Sometimes recognition of the 4th, 3rd, and 2nd string is less familiar for playing purposes, but for reading purposes we need to be just as comfortable reading pitches here.

We will examine all the pitches up to the twelfth fret on every string before reading exercises on single strings. This will help us as we go forward and learn the higher positions on the guitar neck through the remainder of these texts. You will encounter some new pitches on the first string as the fifth position ends on a C above the staff at its highest pitch.

Notes on the 1st String

The notated pitches, frets, and letter names are given to you here in chromatic order. It is imperative to memorize all the information here. A great way to do that is by running through a cycle of 4ths and/or circle of 5ths exercise on the single string. Say the note names aloud as you do this. We will use only flat names in the cycle of 4ths and only sharp names in the circle of 5ths.

The exercises here should be repeated until you are able to get from one to the next accurately and almost instantly. We are using intervals of 4ths and 5ths because they are large leaps. This should help train pitch recognition on the string because you have to travel large distances to get from one pitch to the next. When you are ready, try reading the examples below on the first string only, using any fingering that allows you to access the pitches quickly:

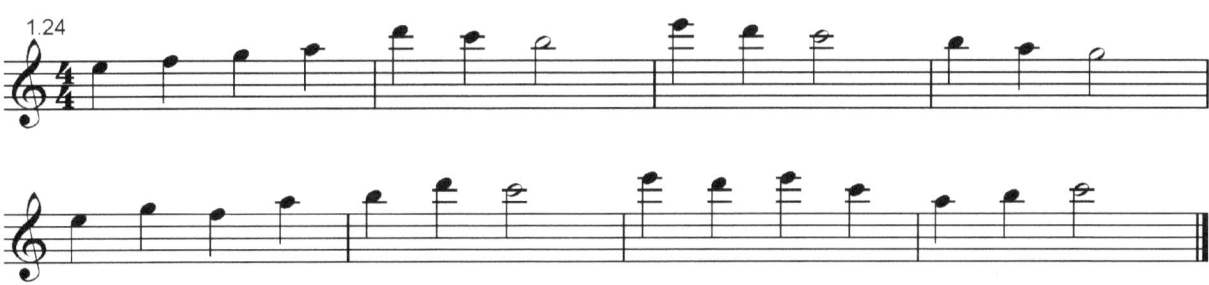

Now read the same example but follow the indicated fingerings:

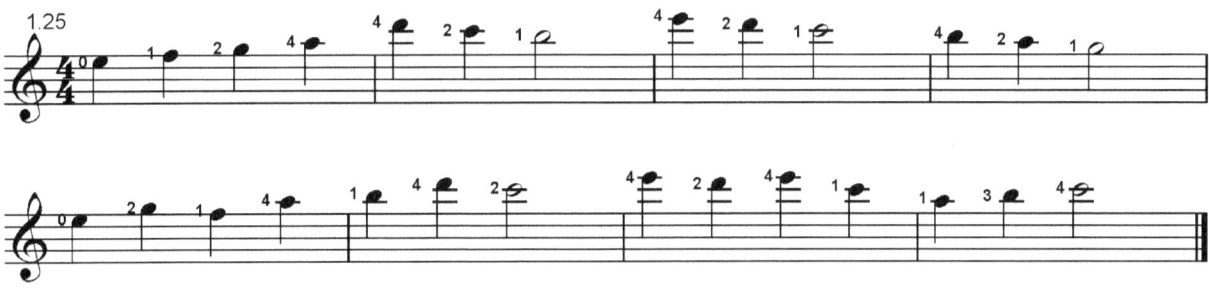

The goal behind the fingerings when playing melodies on a single string is to create the minimum amount of shifts possible. Do not play more than two notes on the same string with the same finger. This rule will prevent frets being missed and sloppy sounding playing. Use stretches to cover more area within a single position but try to avoid stretching between the third and fourth finger when possible. Make sure to keep stretches between the first and second finger whenever you can. *If you don't believe me, take a ruler and measure the distance you can stretch between the third and fourth fingers and compare it to the distance you can*

stretch between the first and second fingers. Unless your name is Paul Gilbert, you will probably find the stretch between the first and second fingers to be significantly longer!

Keeping these fingering ideas in mind, try these examples on the first string only:

*Take advantage of open strings for smooth position shifting.

Notes on the 6th String

Now try the same approach on the 6th string:

The frets and note names are a duplicate of the 1st string here, with the pitches sounding two octaves lower. The only adjustment will be pitch recognition on the staff.

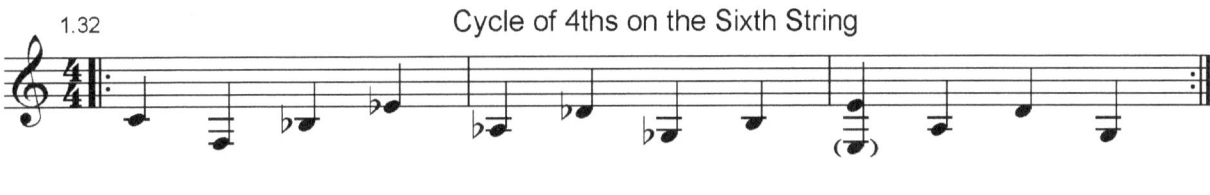

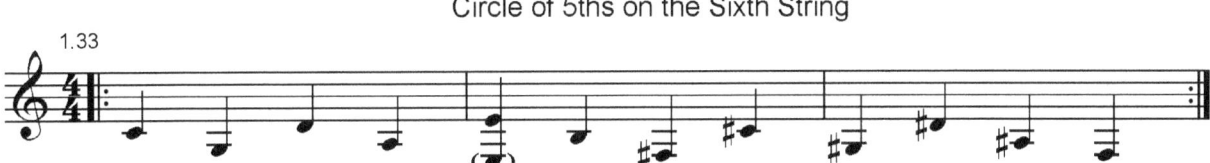

Repeat each over and over until it becomes second nature or try going continuously through both patterns.

1.34

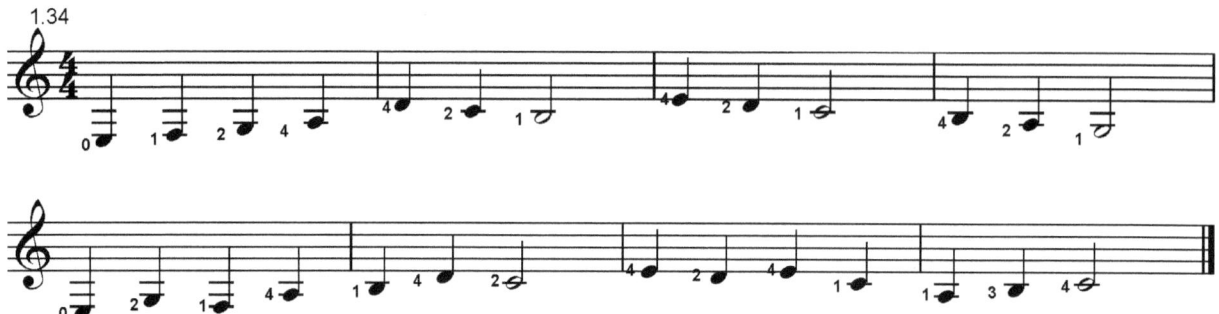

This is the same example down two octaves that began our study of the 1st string. Take note of the suggested finger stretches and apply the concepts to the exercises below:

1.35

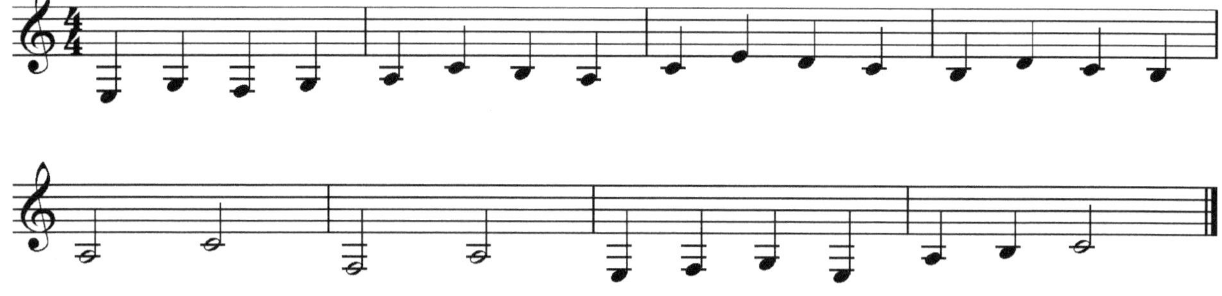

1.36

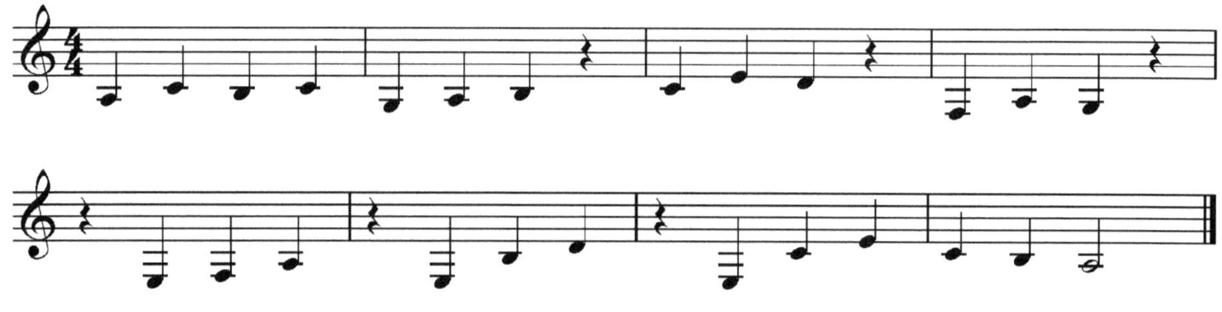

1.37

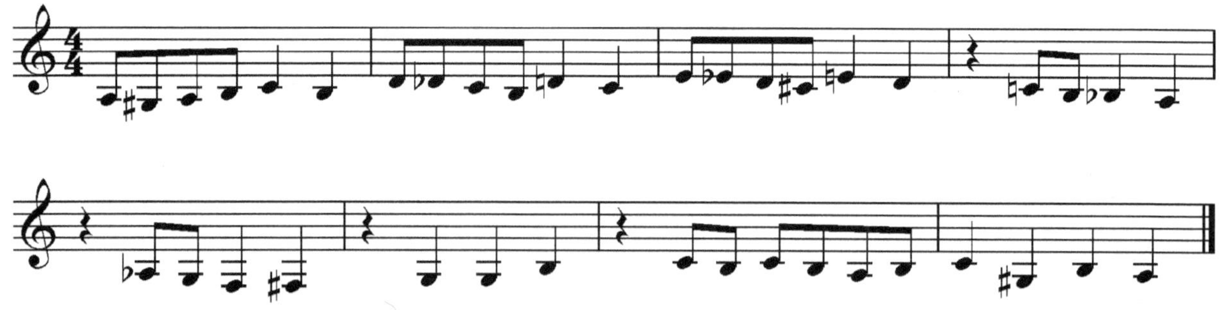

Notes on the 5th String

Cycle of 4ths on the Fifth String

Circle of 5ths on the Fifth String

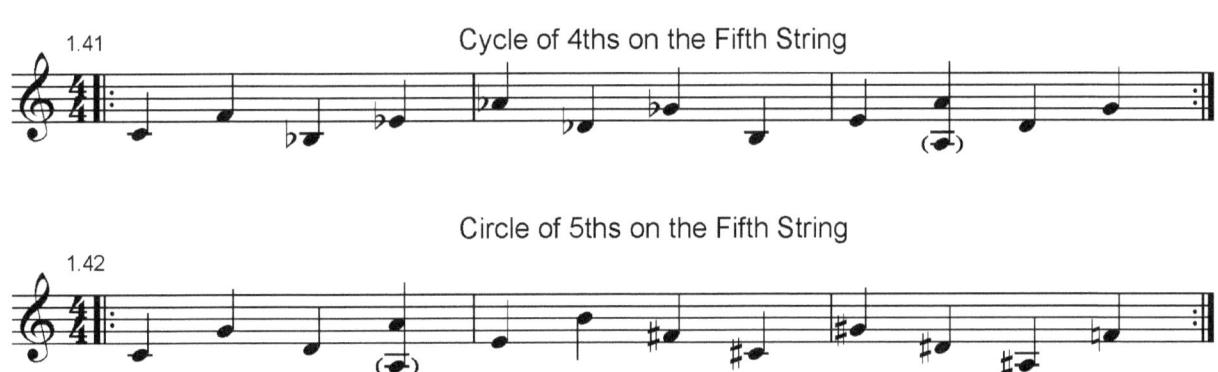

Notes on the 4th String

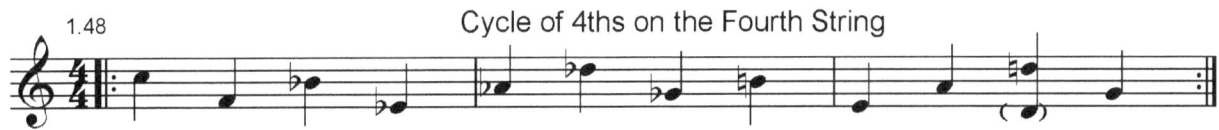

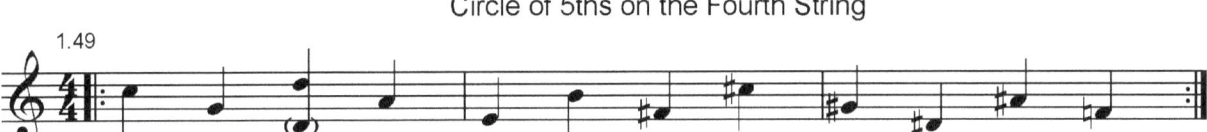

Notes on the 3rd String

1.60

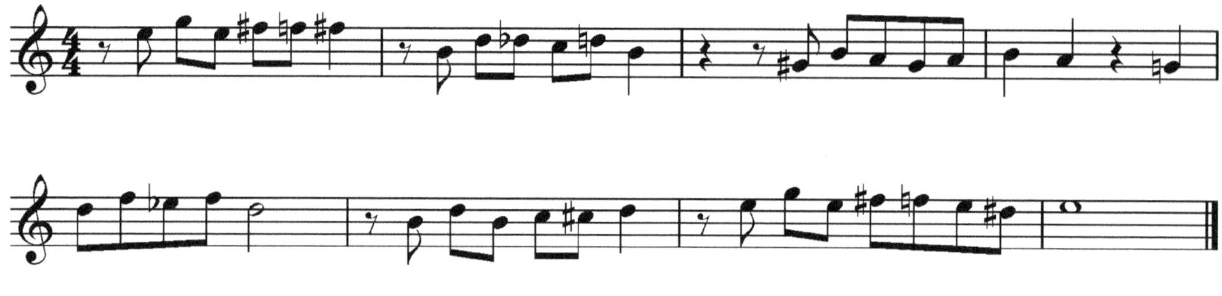

1.61

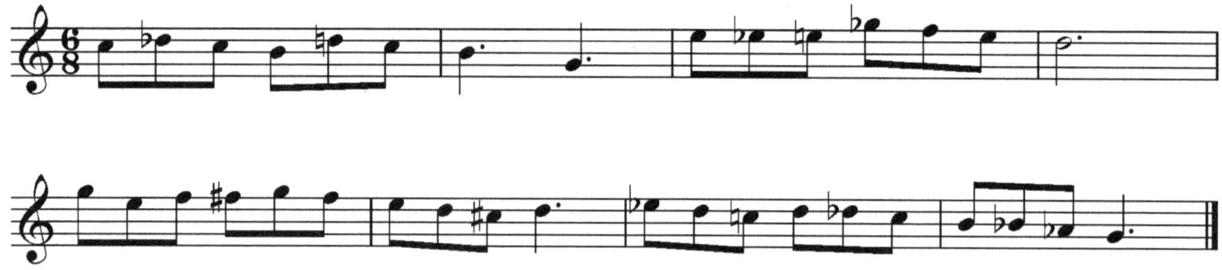

1.62

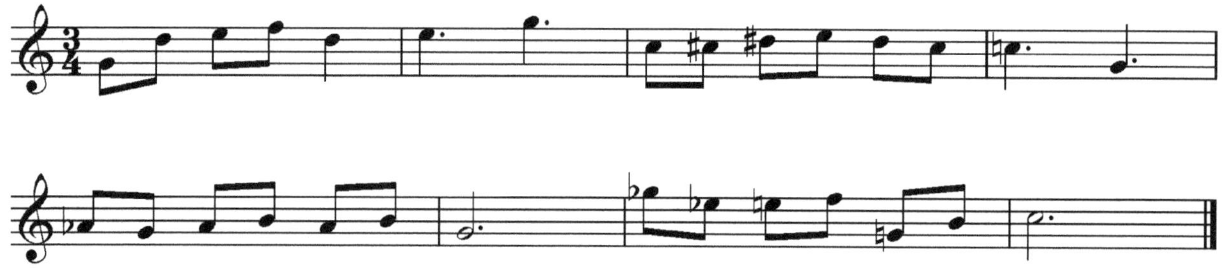

Notes on the 2nd String

1.63

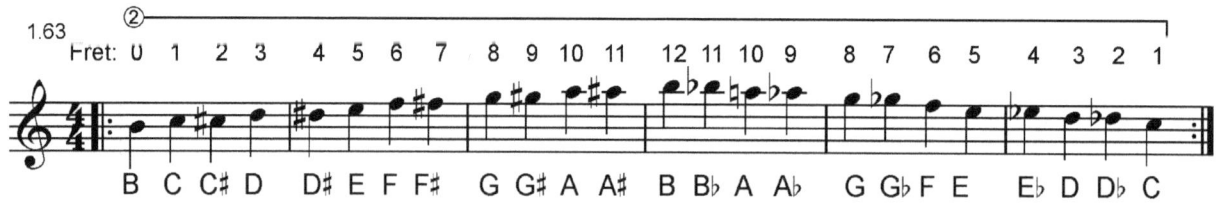

Notes on the 1st String

Assignment:

Si What I Did There?

Chapter 2: Introduction to Position VI, Sixteenth Note Syncopation, and Palm Mutes

Examine position VI and its potential fingerings:

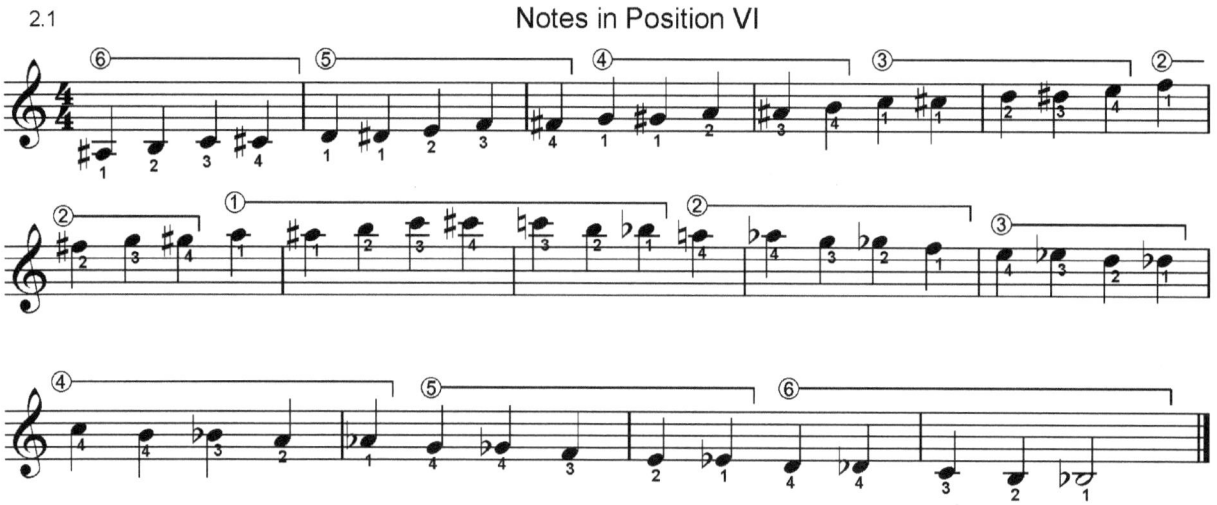

The fingerings here are given in terms of a chromatic scale. It would be perfectly acceptable to use the *enharmonic* fingering to help sculpt a good flow for a given musical passage. In the following exercises the fingering choices will be left up to you. Make sure to stay in position VI as you play these passages:

C Major

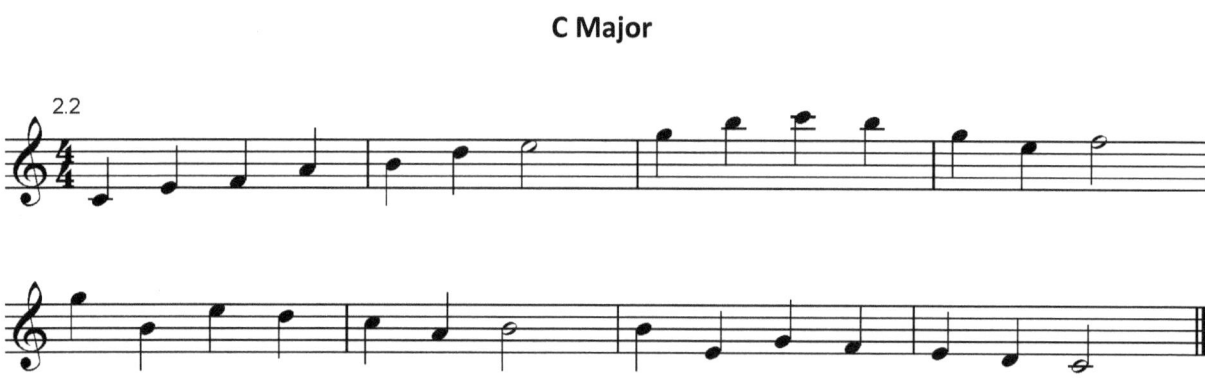

A Minor

F Major

D Minor

Bb Major

G Minor

G Major

E Minor

D Major

B Minor

Sixteenth Note Syncopation

If playing at the eighth note level, the right hand should follow the down/up direction of your foot tap.

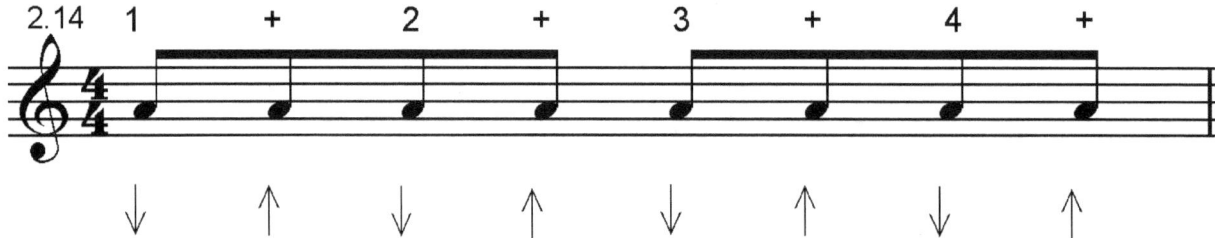

When playing solid sixteenth notes, you should double the speed of your picking. This would mean that all notes on down beats and off beats would be played with a downwards pick direction. All the notes in between (e's and a's) would be played with an upwards pick direction. Therefore you would have two even beat divisions when your foot hits the ground, and two even beat divisions when your foot reaches it's apex.

If eighth notes are included with the sixteenth note rhythms you have two options. If the tempo is slow, keep the down beats and off beats as down strokes:

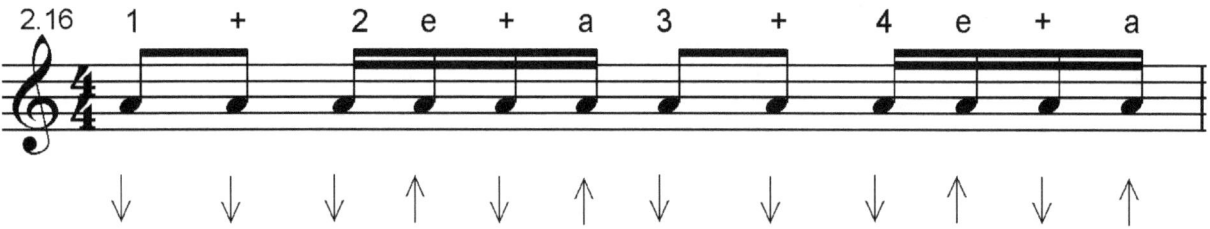

At faster tempos it is probably best to keep eighth notes as down-up picking:

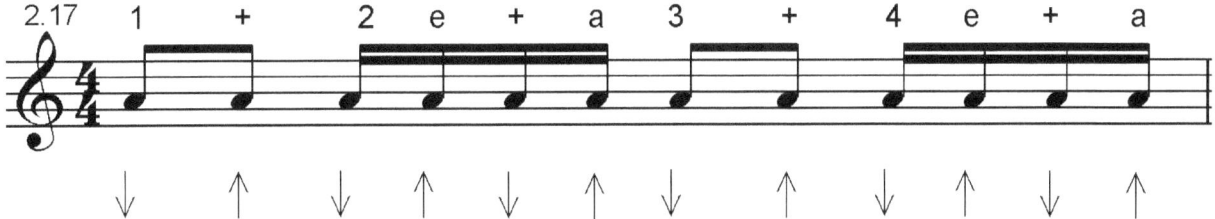

When eighth and sixteenth notes are grouped within the same beat, keep all downbeats and off beats as alternate picking:

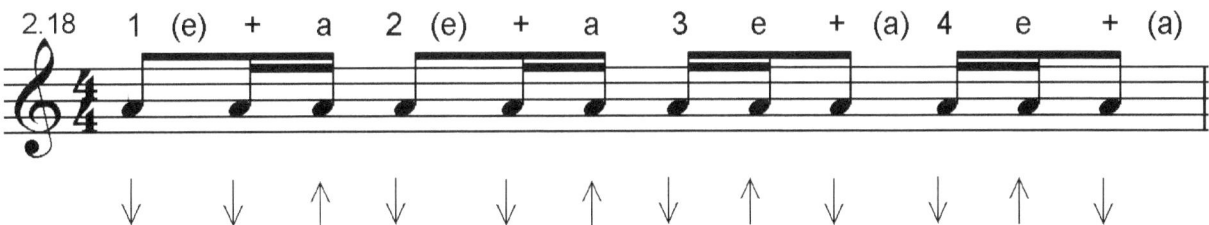

Keep your pick moving up and down off the string in a sixteenth note pulse to help you subdivide and maintain a consistent feel.

Try the following examples. The first will be the same basic rhythm as the next three, with different tie groupings each time:

Here are the same four rhythmic groups with pitches included. Read in any position(s) you would like:

2.23

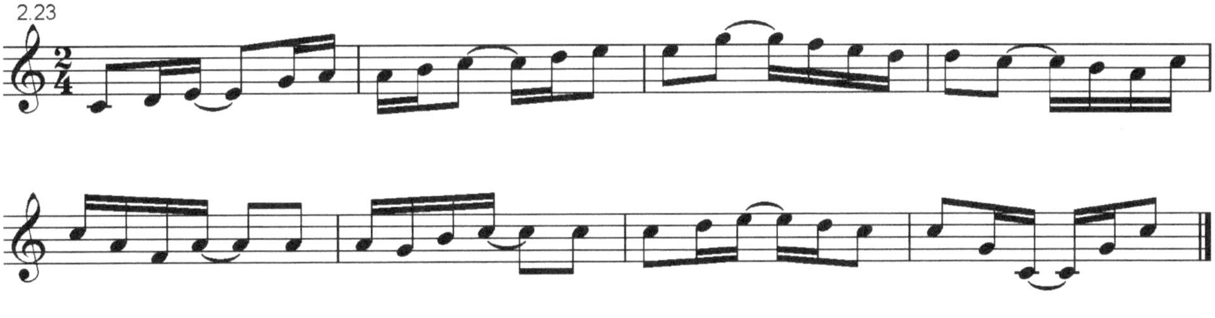

2.24

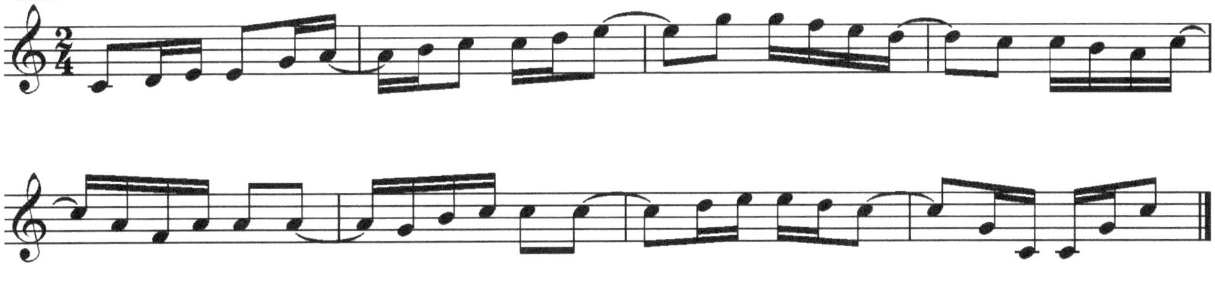

2.25

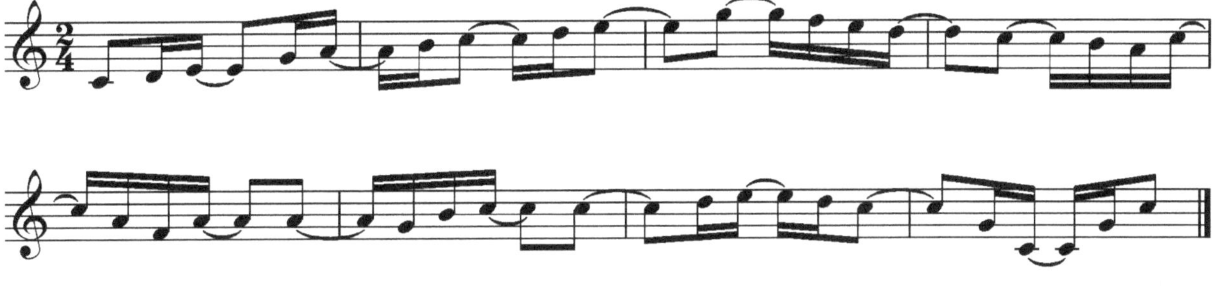

Try the same process throughout the next two pages:

2.26

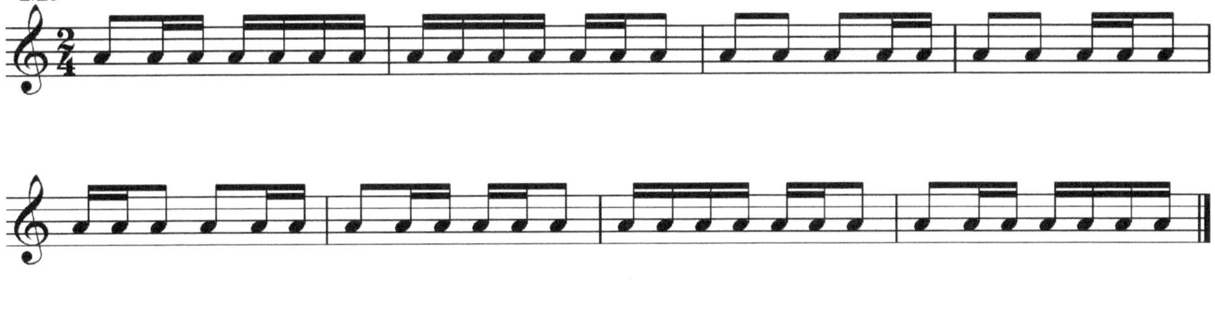

2.31

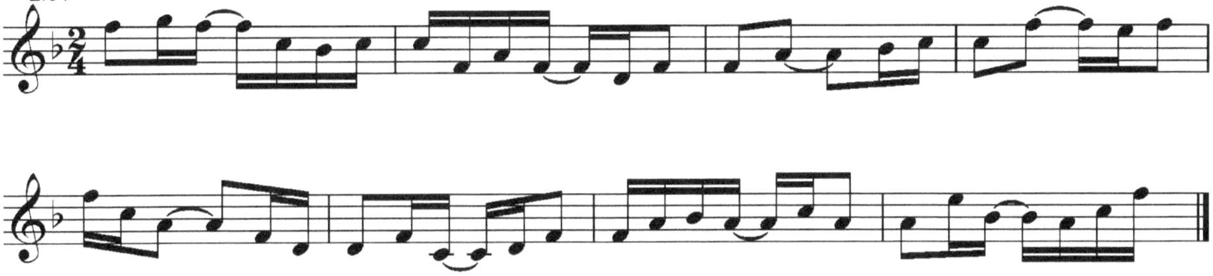

2.32

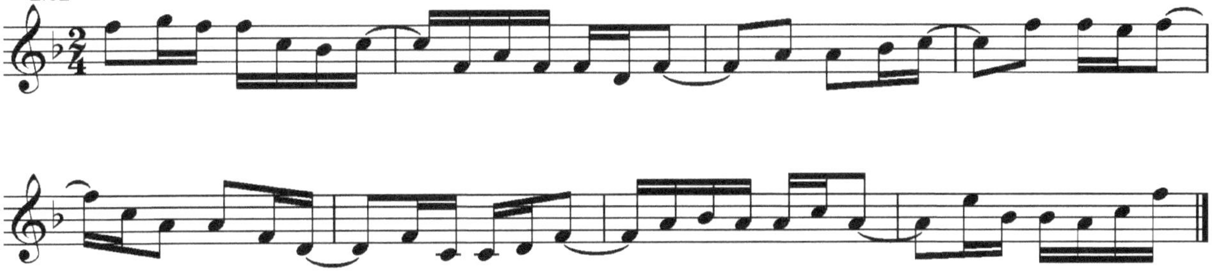

2.33

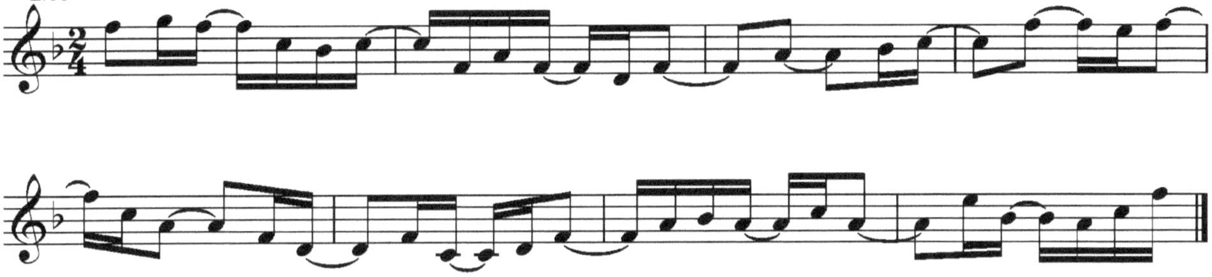

Try it all again but this time with a different meter:

2.34

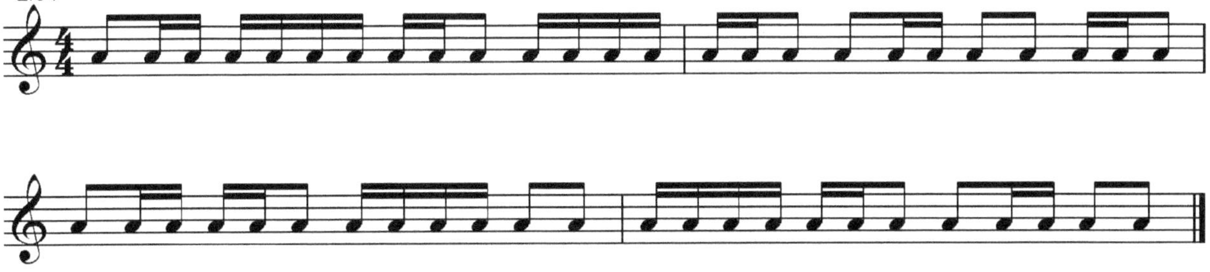

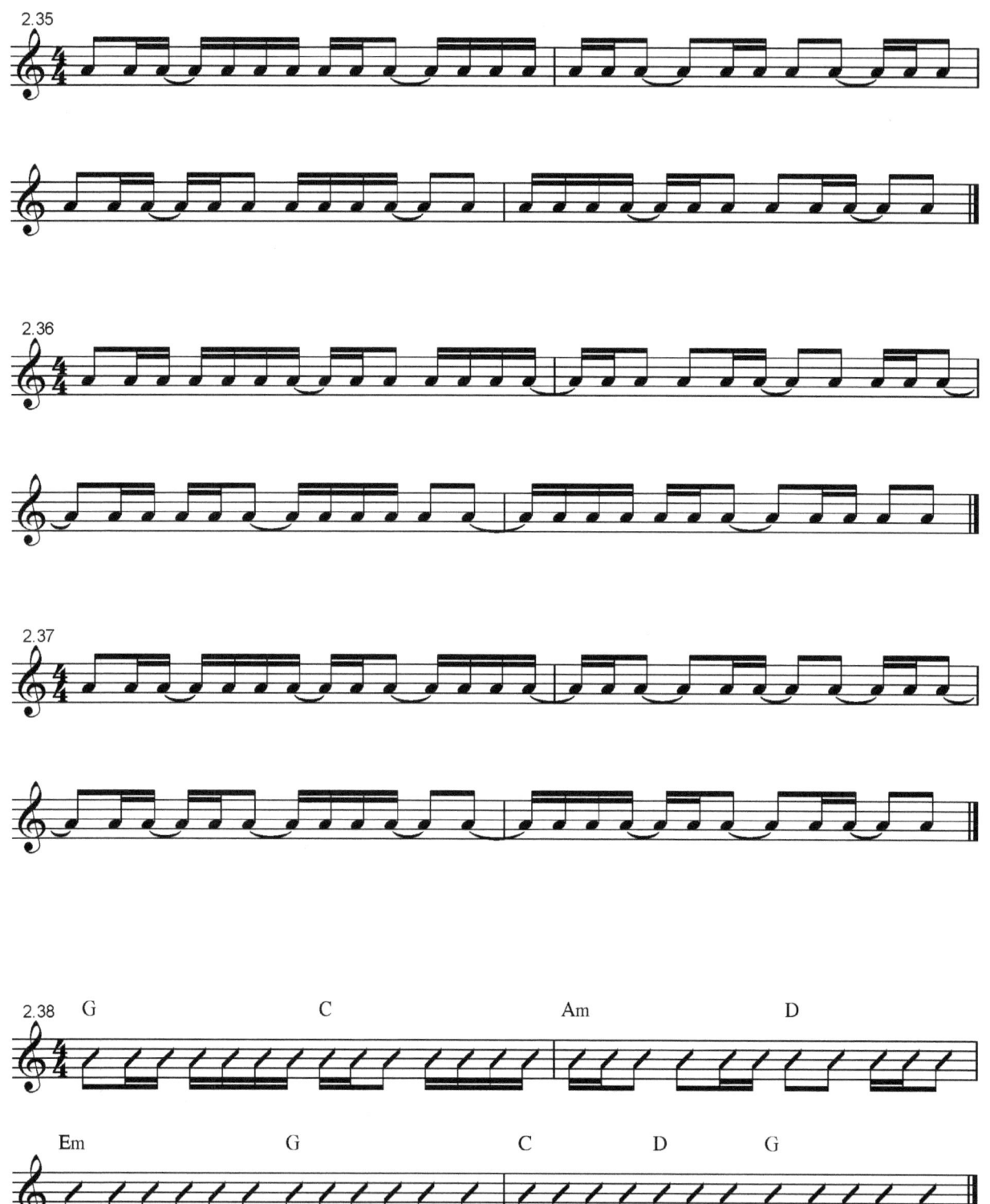

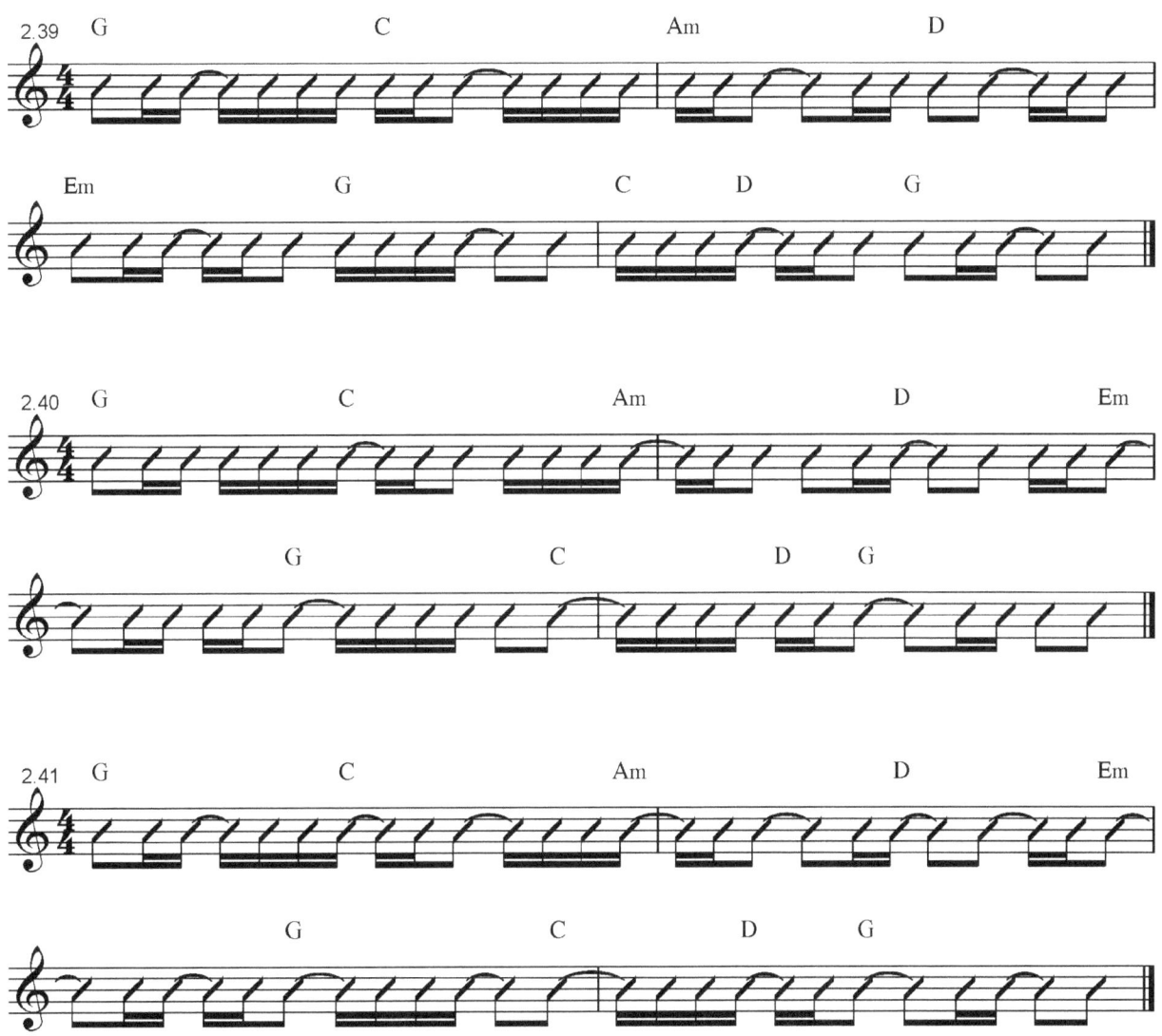

Reading Articulations: Palm Mutes

A palm mute occurs when strings are dampened at the bridge for a less sustained effect. The higher the palm moves off the bridge and up the strings, the more muted the notes become. There is no nomenclature to instruct the performer as to how muted the sound should be, and typically would rely on the players intuition. In some cases, written instructions may be given in cases of extreme or light palm muting.

Try these exercises in any position, taking care to apply and remove palm mutes. Do not overdo the effect:

Assignment:

The Entrepreneurial Blacksmith
(He Who Smelt It Dealt It)

Chapter 3: Position VI and Sixteenth Note Syncopation Continued, Let Ring

Continue to read in position VI:

F Minor

Db Major

Bb Minor

A Major

F# Minor

E Major

C# Minor

B Major

G# Minor

Sixteenth Note Syncopation Continued

Let us continue our study of sixteenth note syncopation by focusing on three new rhythmic subdivisions and their proposed picking directions:

Keep your pick moving in a continuous down-up motion in the air off the string when longer note values occur.

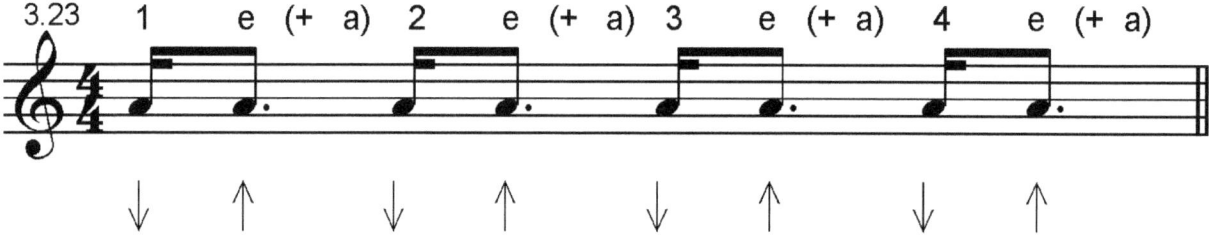

Try the following examples. The first will be the same basic rhythm as the next three, with different tie groupings each time:

45

Here are the same four rhythmic groups with pitches included. Read in any position(s) you would like:

Try the same process throughout the next group of examples combining the rhythmic groups from this chapter with those of chapter 2:

Sixteenth Note Syncopation in 6/8 Time

Remember that when there is an 8 in the denominator, the sixteenth notes in 6/8 time would be counted and picked the same way as we would if they were eighth notes in time signatures with a 4 in the denominator:

3.40

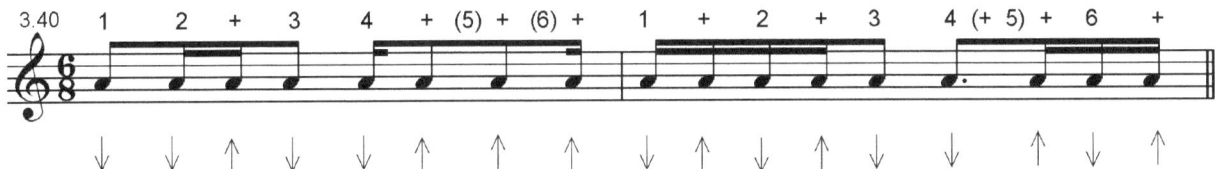

Try the following exploration of 6/8 syncopation:

3.41

3.42

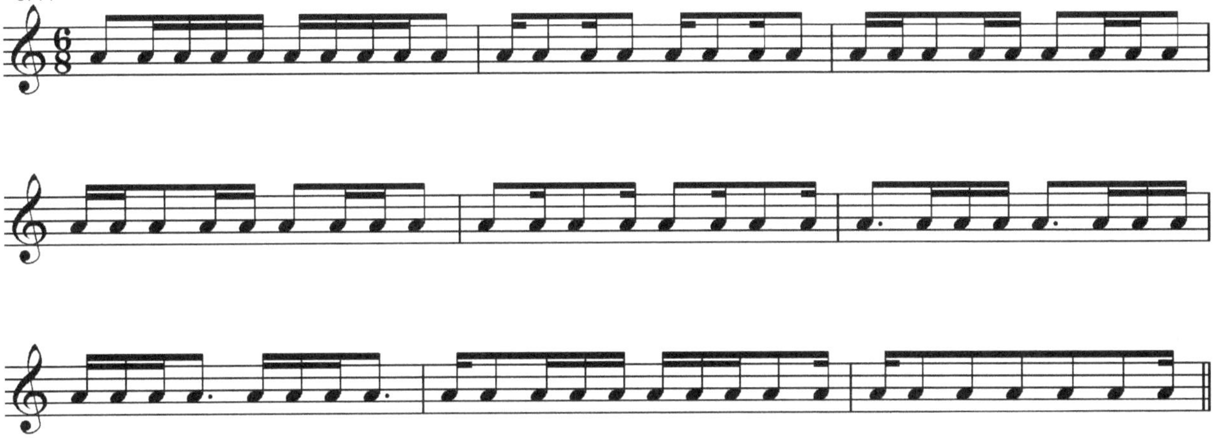

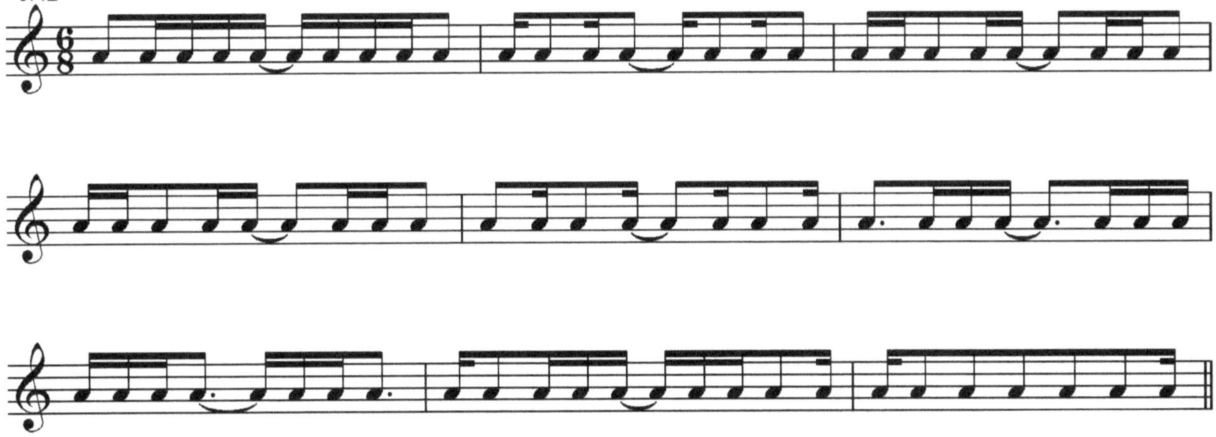

Reading Articulations: Let Ring

You will often find passages of arpeggiated chords written with a *let ring* notation. This would indicate you should let each pitch sound for as long as possible before silencing. You would commonly use open strings as much as possible to achieve the desired effect, although this may be written with barred chords as well.

Try the following *let ring* examples:

This page has been left blank intentionally

Assignment:

Chapter 4: Position VI, Horizontal Reading and Sixteenth Note Funk Articulations

Continue to read in position VI:

Gb Major

Eb Minor

Cb Major

Ab Minor

F# Major

D# Minor

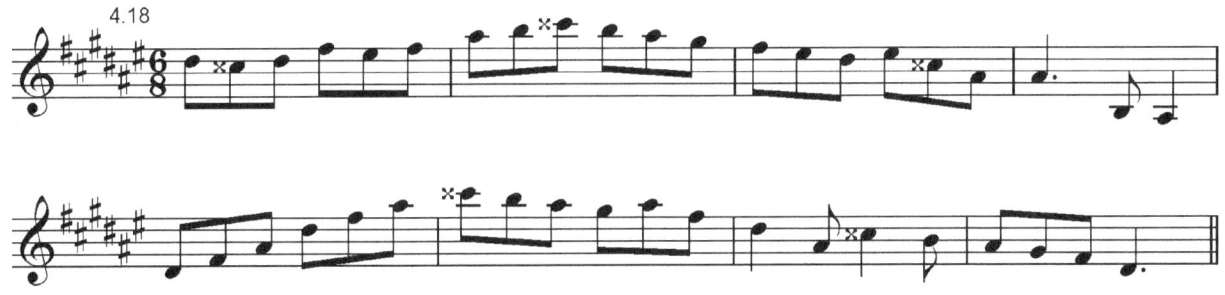

C# Major

A# Minor

Horizontal Reading

Read each passage in the indicated positions. Each exercise focuses on two strings only:

Sixteenth Note Funk Articulations

We will now look at specific funk articulations, specifically muted attacks. Muted attacks are written with a "x" notation. They imply the player should lighten the pressure of the left hand so that a percussive *thud* sound is produced and not an actual pitch. The right hand should continue to flow in the *down-up-down-up* flow of 16th notes. Maintain the same picking velocity so that there is no change in volume with regular and scratch attacks.

When written in slash notation, you will typically see one "x" in the middle of the staff:

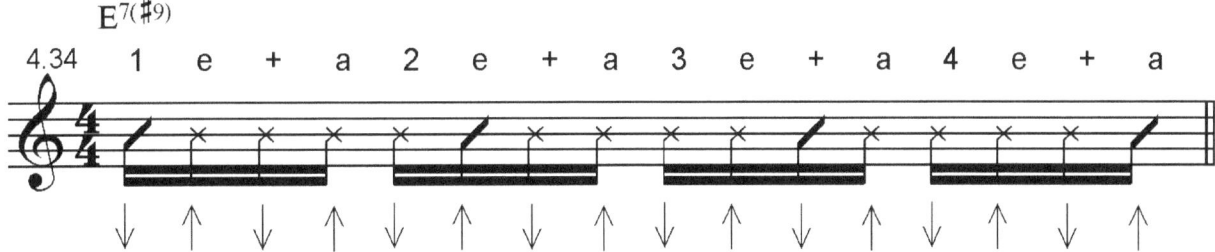

When fully notated chords are provided, you will see the "x" notation written on the same lines that the chord you are using is written on:

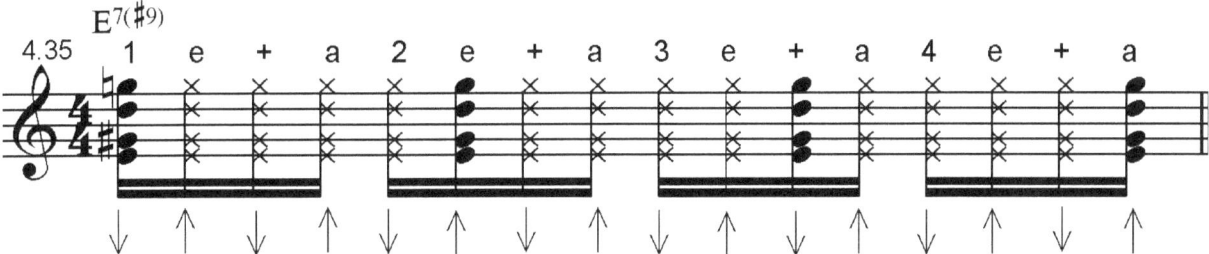

You might also see slides written:

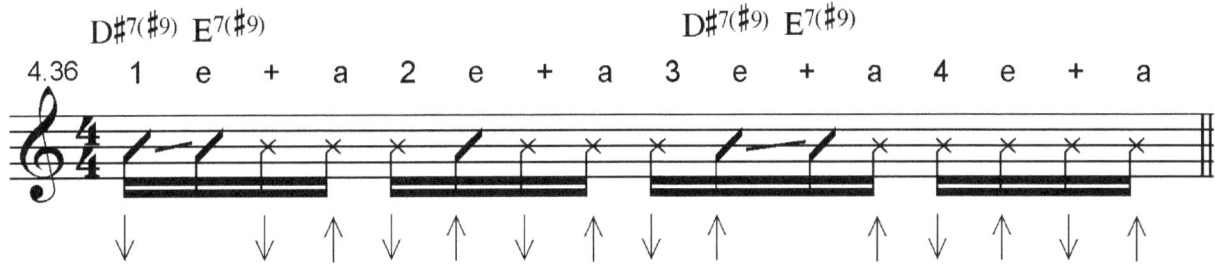

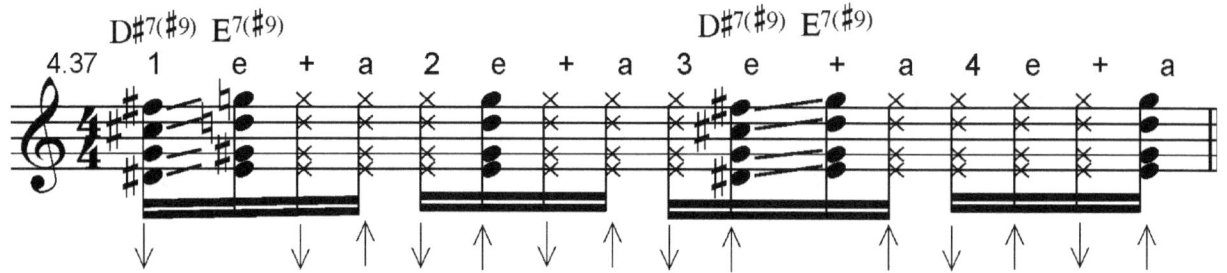

It is also possible to see single note "bubble" or "skank" picking patterns written:

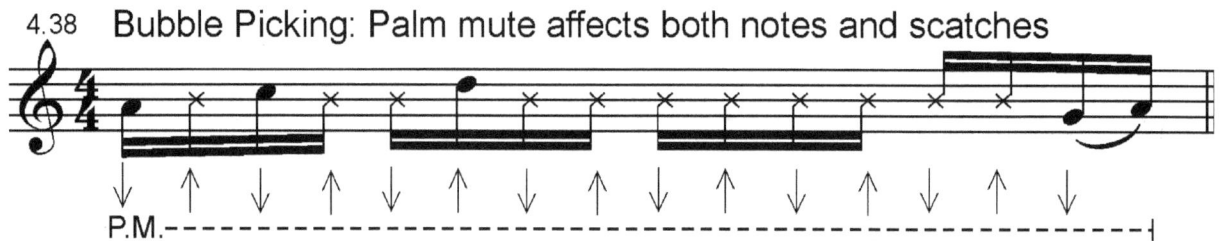

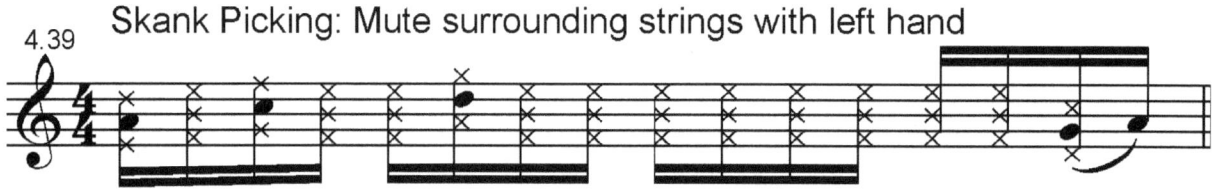

Try the following scratch notation exercises:

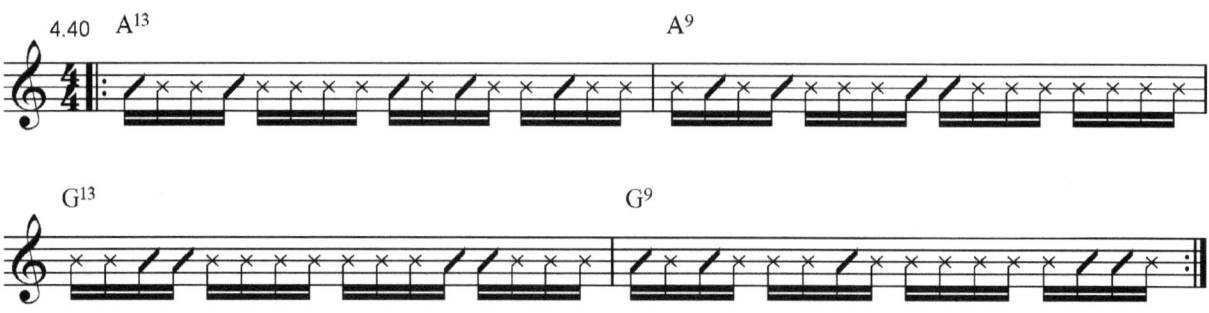

This page has been left blank intentioanlly

Assignment:

Funk King

Chapter 5: Introduction to Position VII, Sixteenth Note Syncopation with rests, and Counterpoint Reading in Position 1

Position VII is one of the most important positions on the guitar neck. It allows access to pitches up to a high D or E (with a stretch) while maintaining a resonant timbre. It also provides friendly fingerings for commonly found keys.

Examine position VII and its potential fingerings:

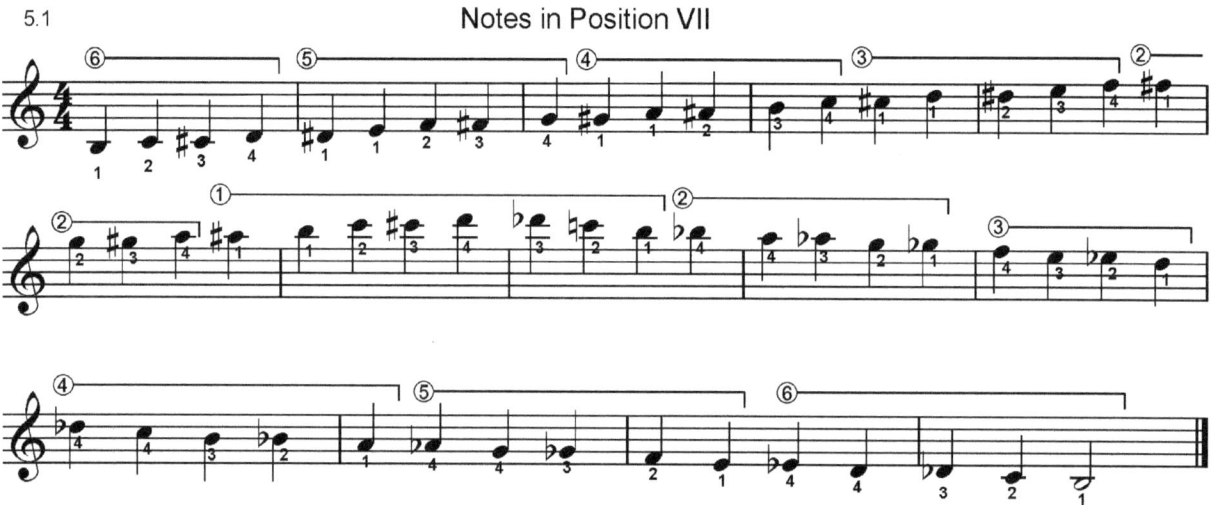

In the following exercises the fingering choices will be left up to you. Make sure to stay in position VII as you play these passages:

C Major

A Minor

F Major

5.12

D Minor

5.13

5.14

Bb Major

5.15

G Minor

G Major

E Minor

D Major

B Minor

Sixteenth Note Rest Syncopation

Let us examine all the potential placements of rests if applied to the rhythms we found in chapters 2 and 3. Try looping the following 4/4 figures:

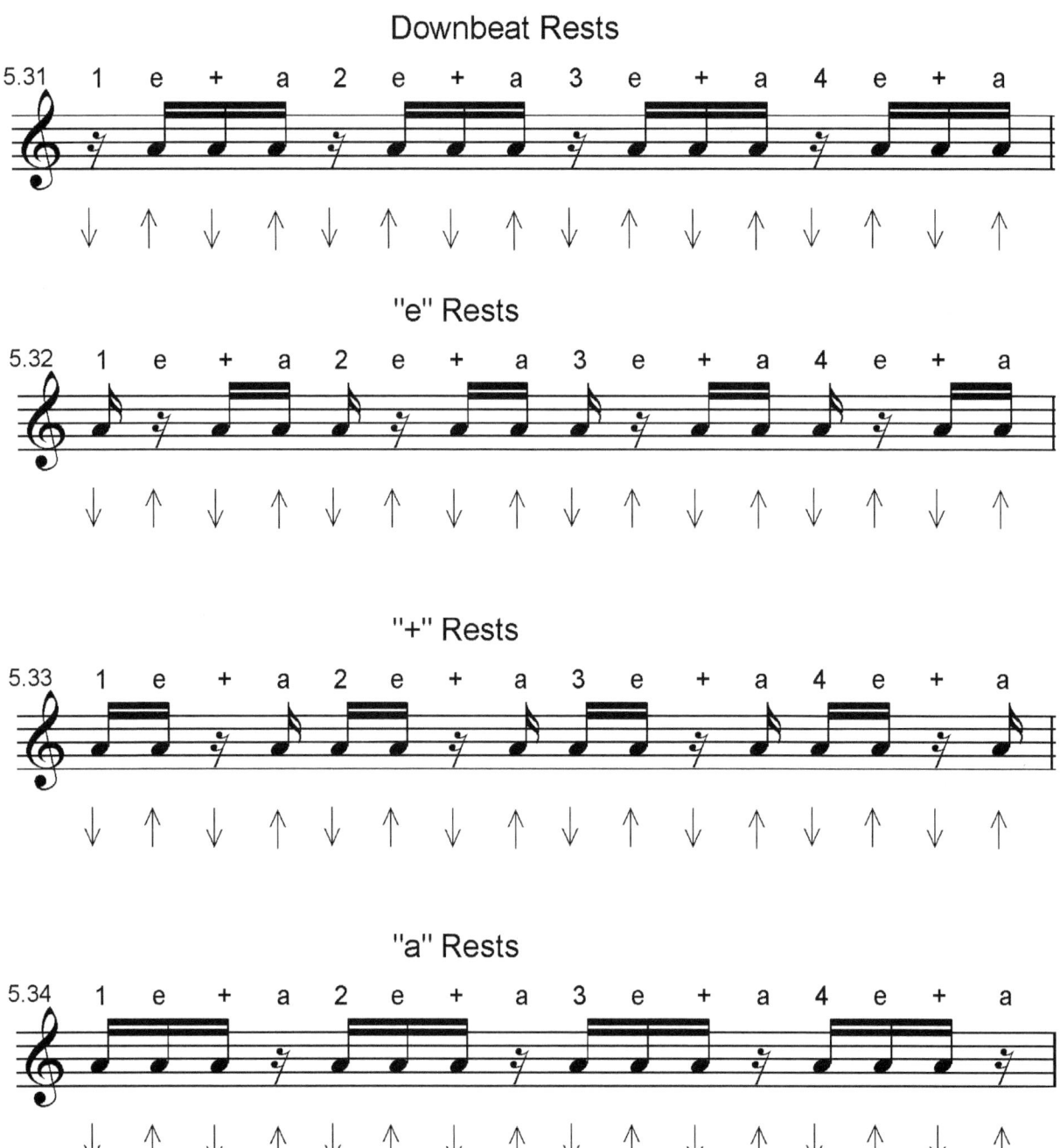

Make sure to mute your sound during the rests or you risk turning the rhythms into some of the combined 8th and 16th note figures we have seen previously.

Here are some possible outcomes when 8th note rests are included with 16th notes.

5.35

5.36

5.37

5.38

5.39

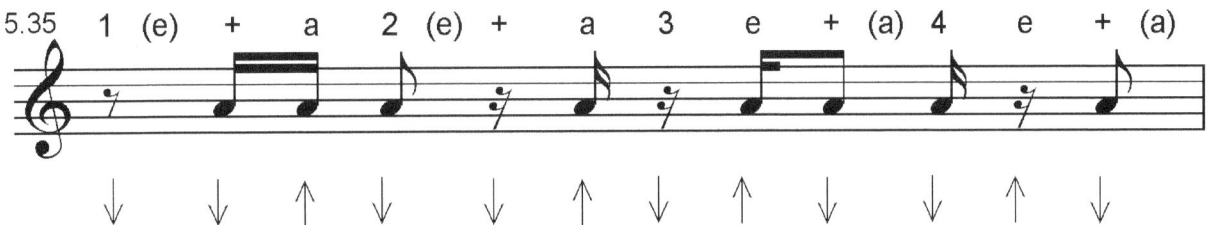

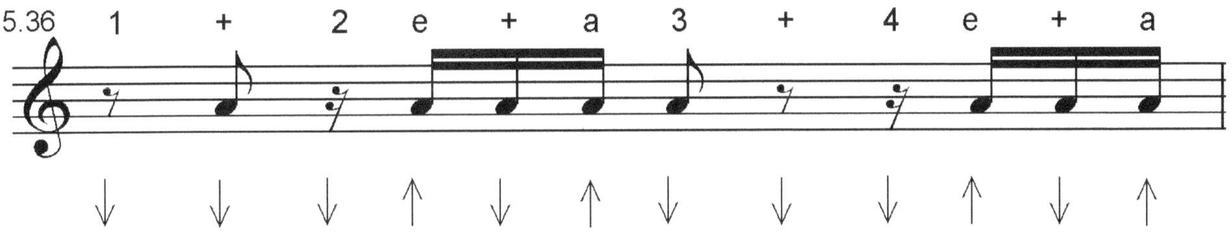

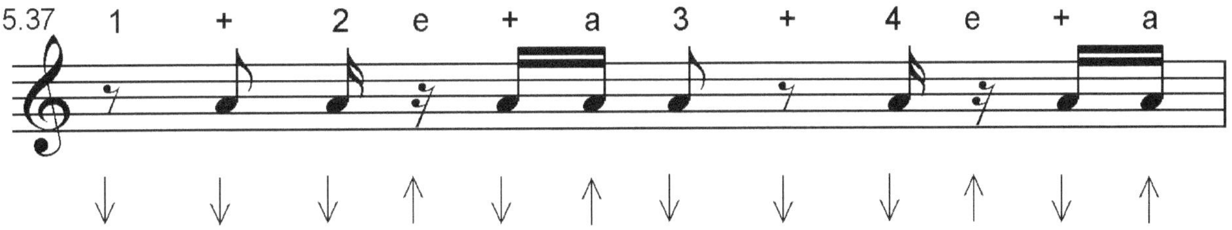

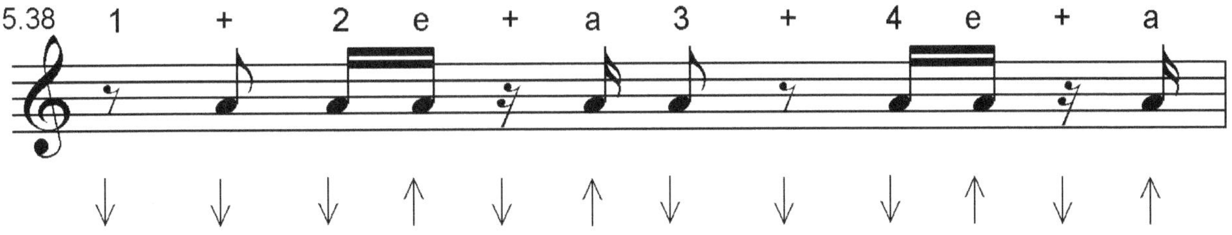

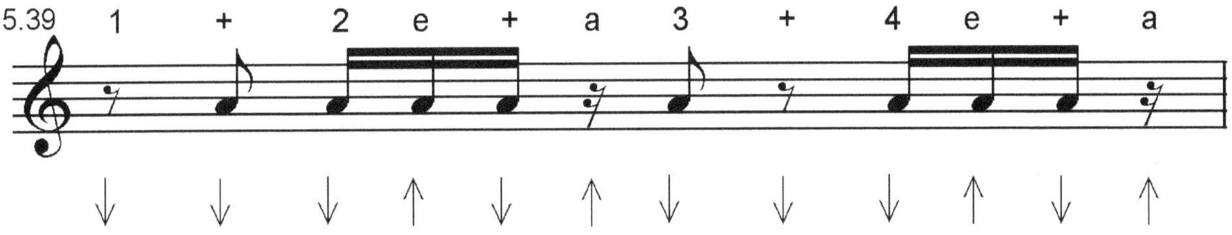

Try the following melodic examples in positions V and/or VII:

Counterpoint in Position I

The term *counterpoint* refers to multiple melodic voices that share the same harmonic concept but move with different rhythms and directions. When performing these examples on the guitar, try to imagine how a pianist would play separate lines with their left and right hands, or how two monophonic instrumentalists might play together. Do your best to make the lines sounds distinct from one another. The up or downwards direction of the stems are a visual guide as to the lower and upper registers of the counterpoint.

Employ open strings as often as possible as you try the following exercises in position I. Make sure that all notes ring out for their full values:

Assignment:

EXPERIMENTING WITH MULTIPLE POSITIONS

Chapter 6: Position VII Continued, Tied Sixteenth Note Syncopation, and Counterpoint Reading in Position I Continued

Let us continue our study of Position VII as you play the following exercises:

Eb Major

C Minor

Ab Major

F Minor

Db Major

Bb Minor

A Major

F# Minor

E Major

6.12

6.13

C# Minor

6.14

B Major

6.15

G# Minor

Sixteenth Note Rest and Tie Syncopation

Maintain a consistent picking for the following examples. Play the melodic examples in Position VII:

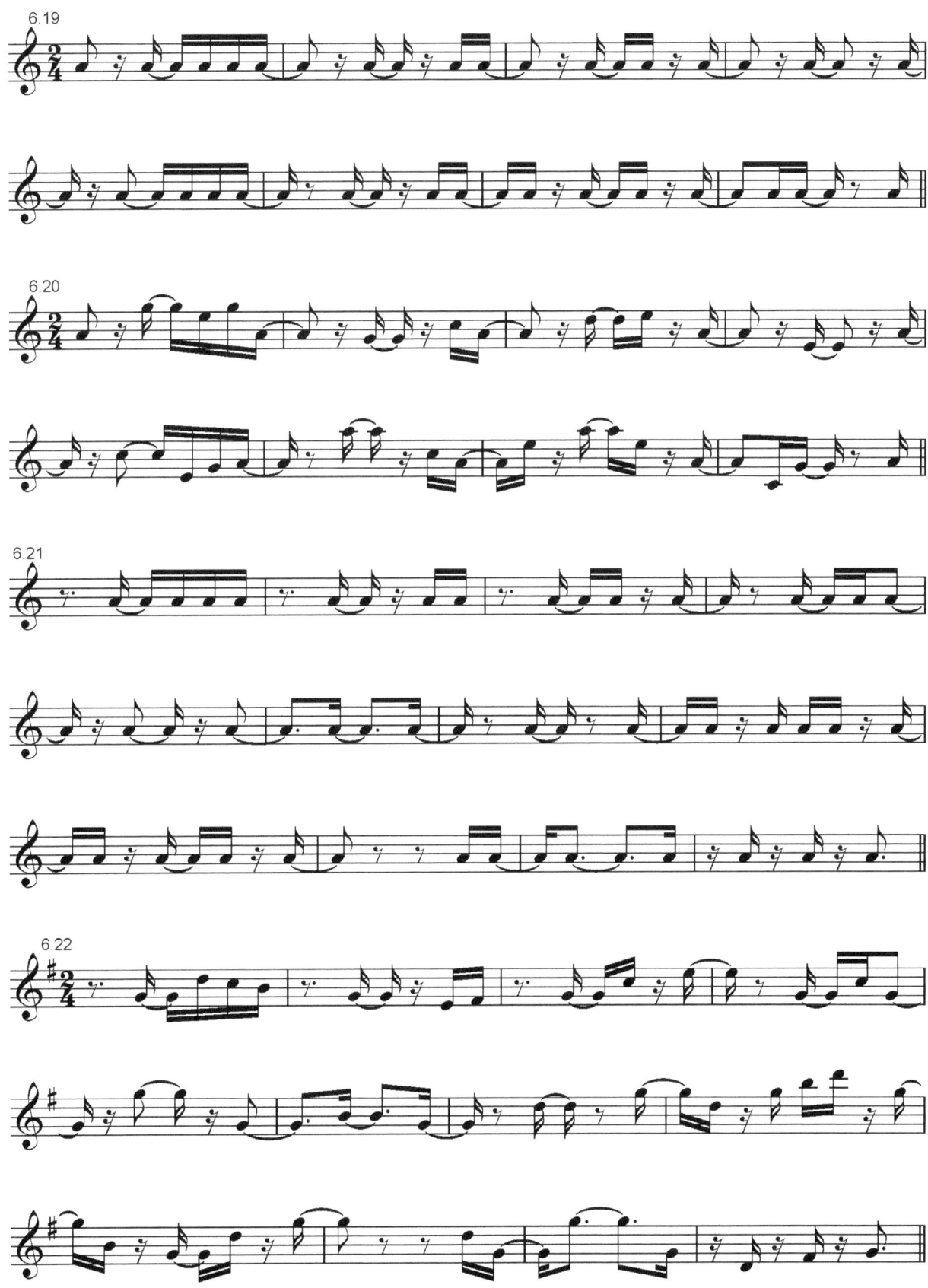

6.25

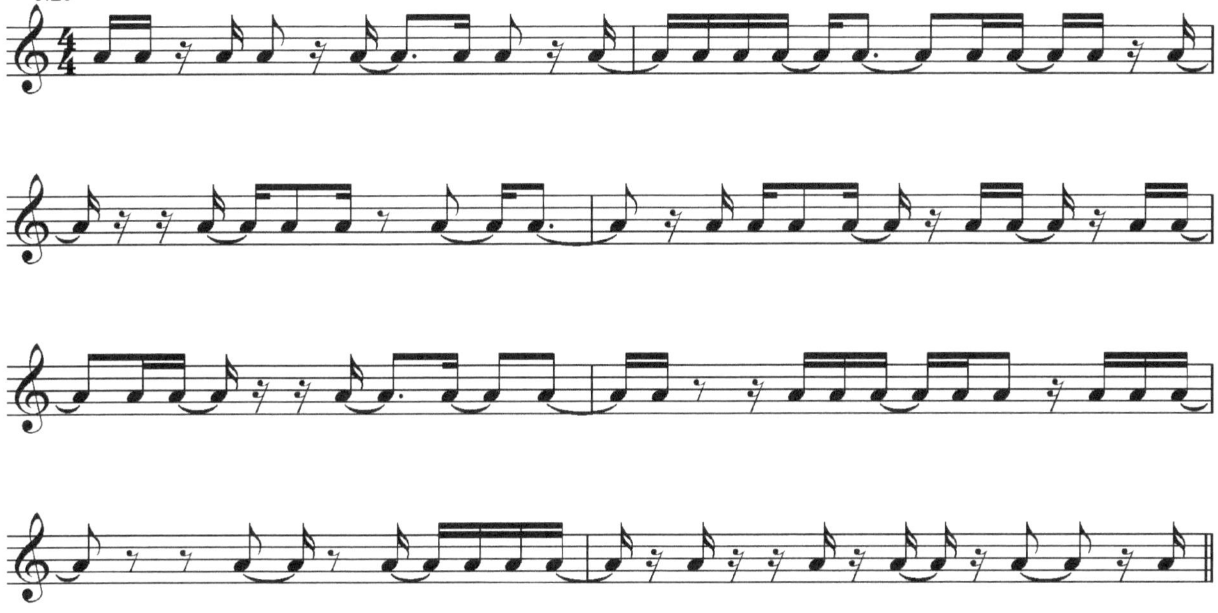

6.26

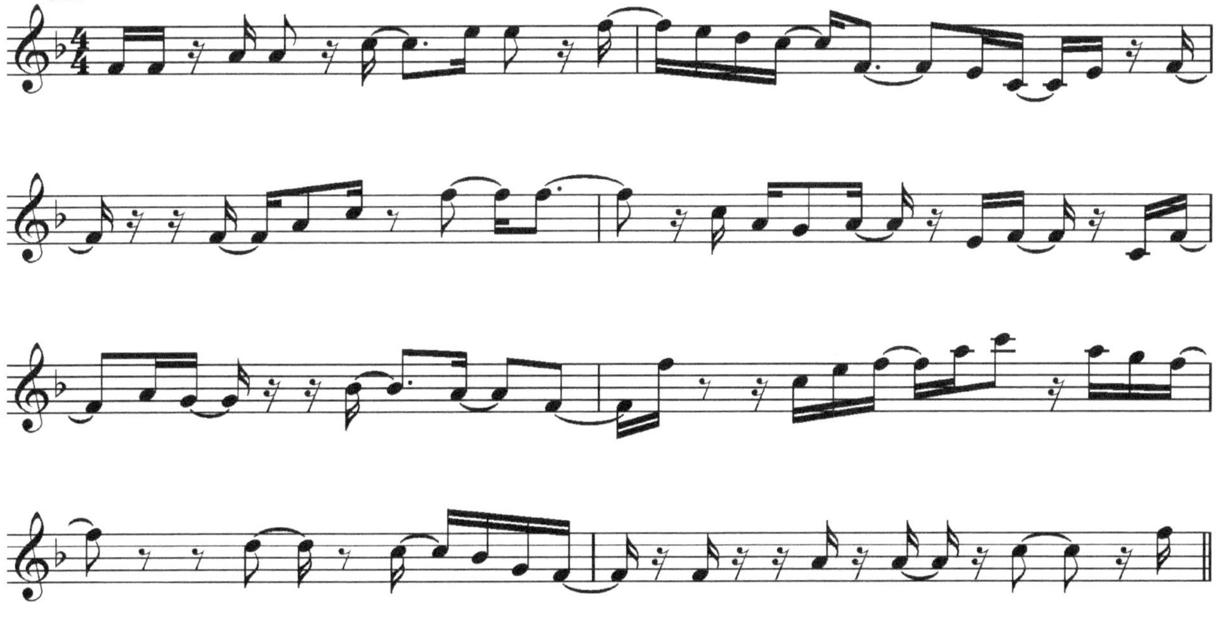

16th Note Reading in 6/8

Since 8th notes are counted as beats in 6/8, simply count the 16th notes as “+”’s.

6.27

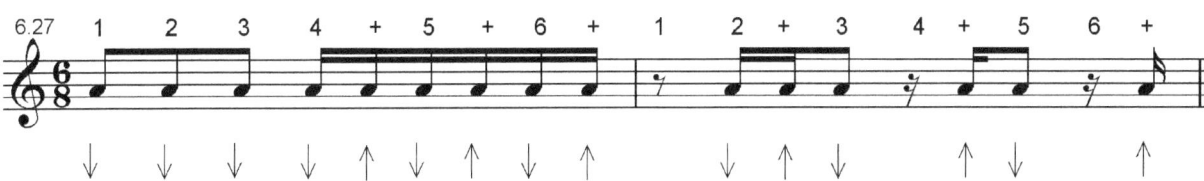

Take these exercises very slowly at first. Set your metronome so that the beat represents the 8th note:

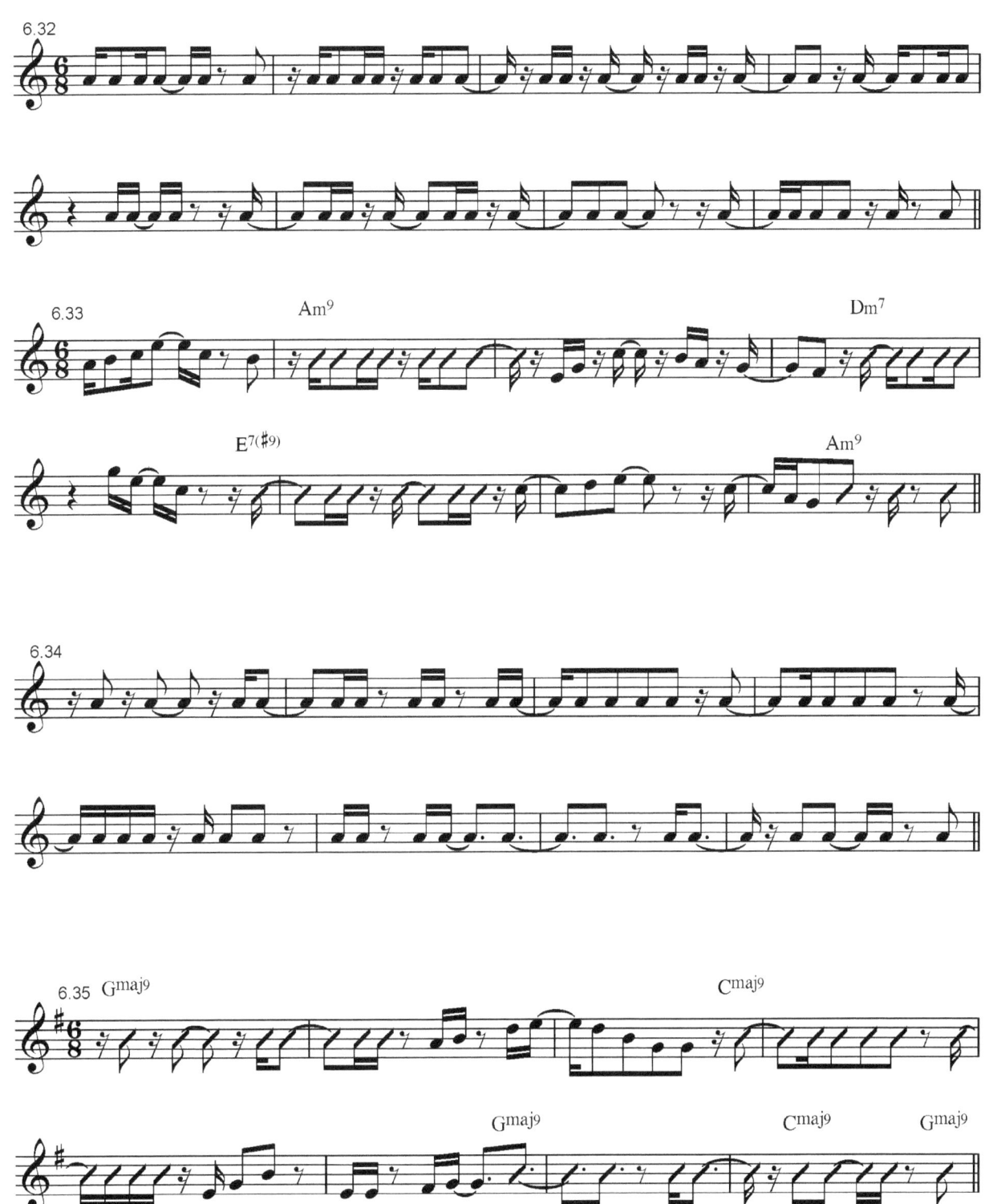

Counterpoint Reading Continued

Read the following exercises in position I:

Assignment:

The Wish Redacting Genie: Rubbed The Wrong Way

Chapter 7: Position VII Continued, Counterpoint Reading in Position II, and Bends

Play the following exercises in position VII:

Ab Minor

F# Major

D# Minor

C# Major

A# Minor

7.8

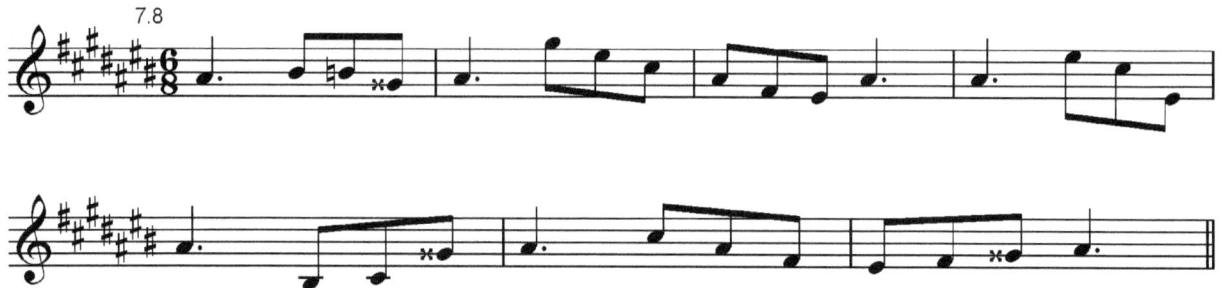

Temporary Modulation

The following exercises will feature phrases that modulate to different keys than the indicated key signatures. Read all pitches in position VII:

7.9

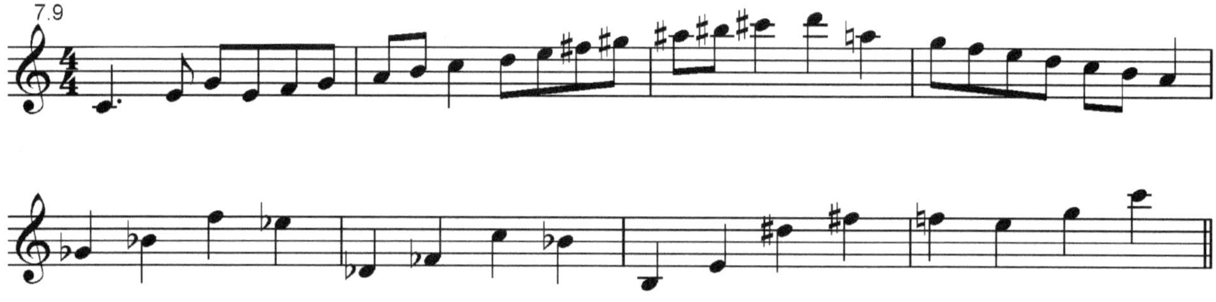

7.10

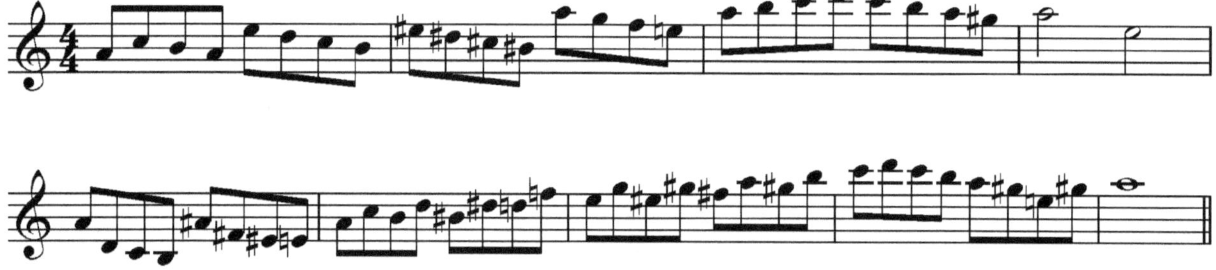

7.11

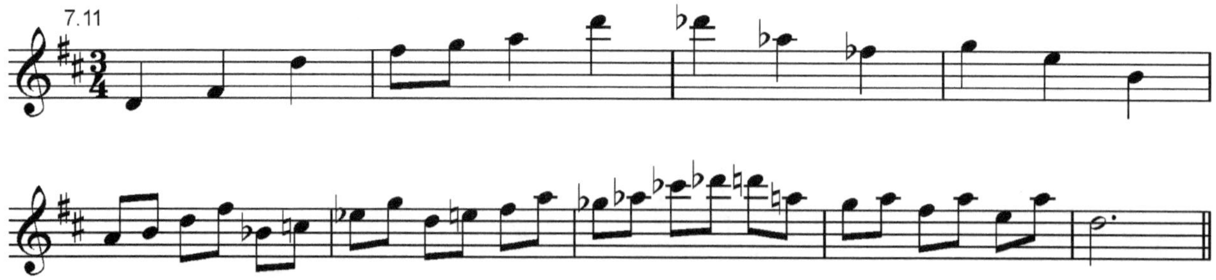

7.12

In the next group of exercises, shift between positions VII and VI when the phrase would dictate an easier fingering in a given position:

7.13

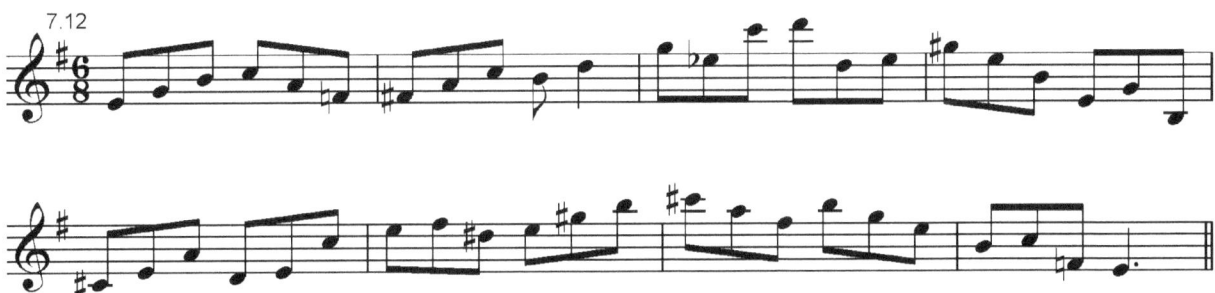

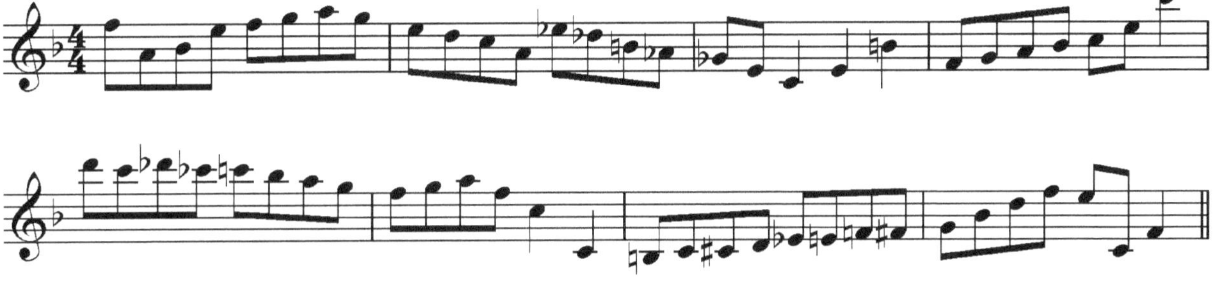

7.14

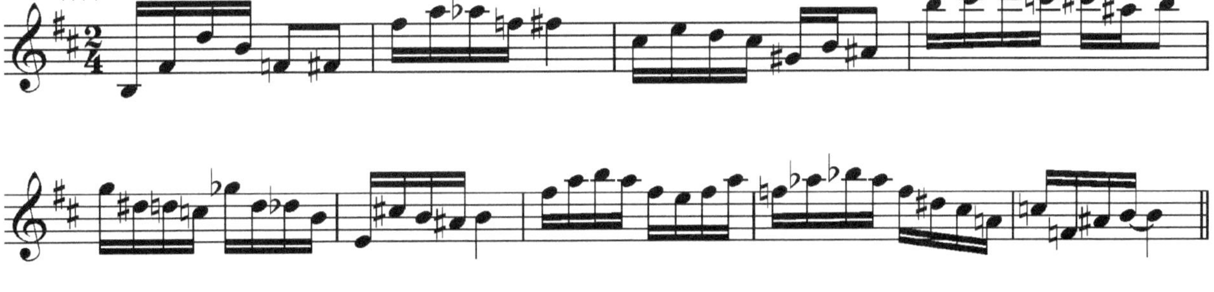

7.15

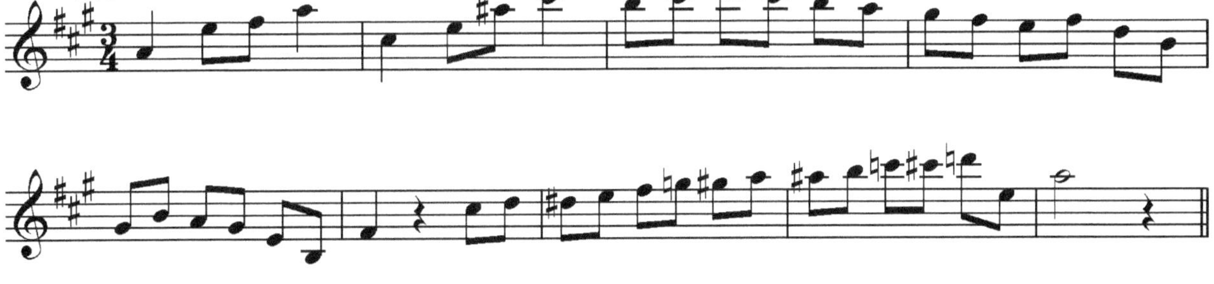

7.20

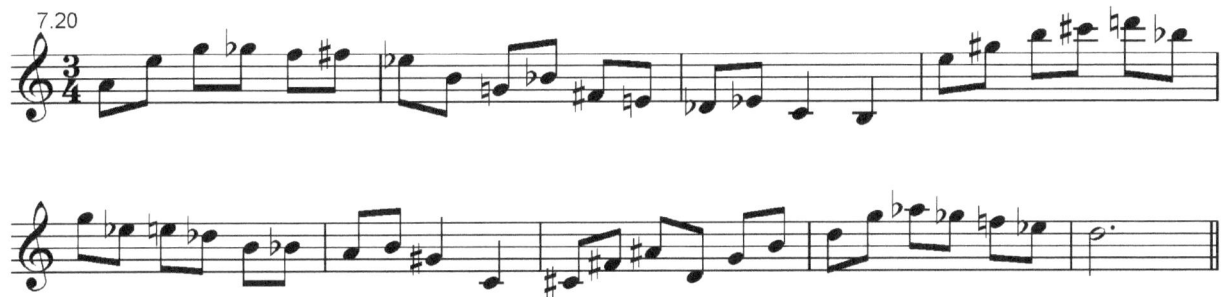

Counterpoint Reading in Position II

Stay in position II as you read the following:

7.21

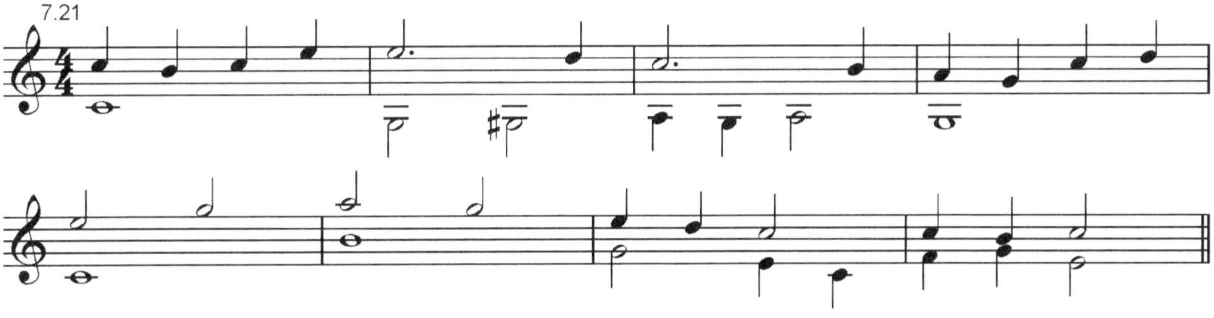

7.22

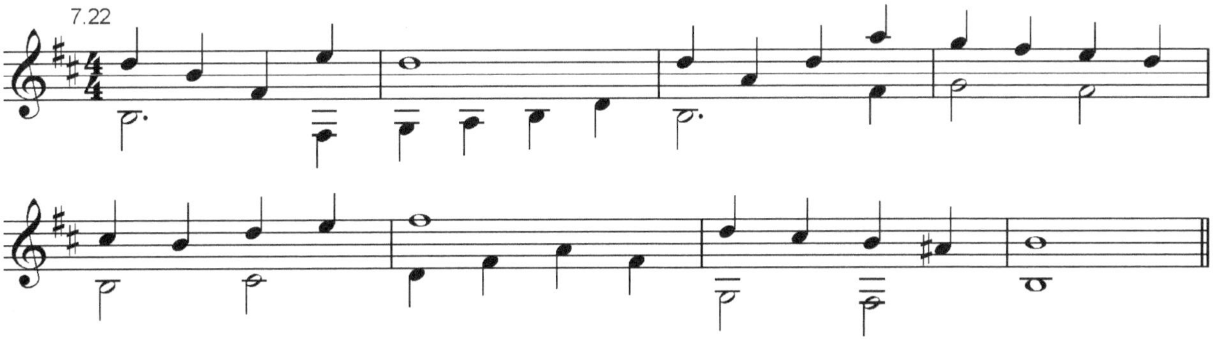

7.23

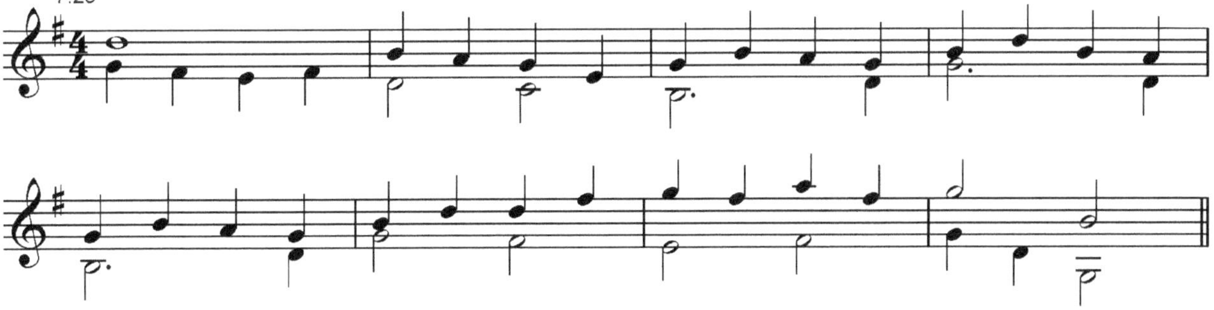

111

Reading Articulations: Bends

Much like reading slides, there are two types of bends you will see notated. A *valued bend* and a *non-valued* bend:

The valued bend would be counted by the attack at beginning of the rhythm. The second pitch would be reached by bend according to the indicated rhythmic value.

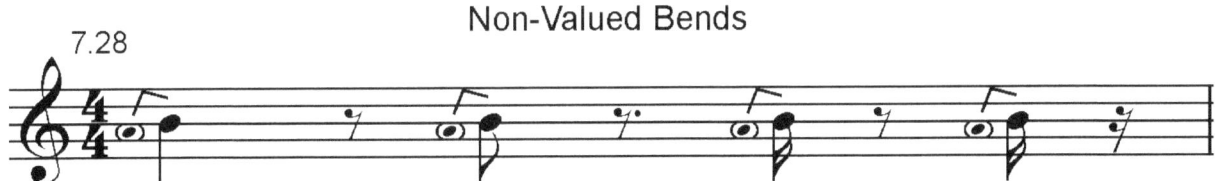

The non-valued bend will occur a pace based on the player's discretion. The bend would begin on the indicated beat on the A note in parenthesis and end on the written pitch B. This is considered a whole step bend. The following are bend distances you might encounter:

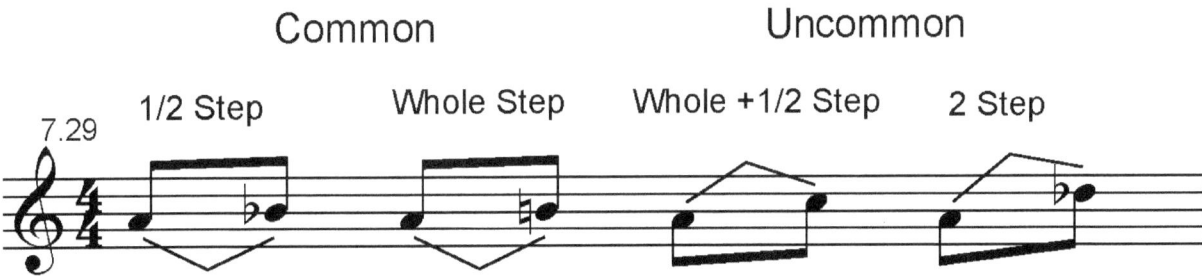

Bend notation can also indicate a *release* or return to the original pitch:

A *pre-bend* is indicated when the string is already bend to the indicated pitch before attacking it. It is typically followed by a release to a lower note:

Valued bends might stop on multiple pitches along the way:

Perform the following exercises in position V:

Bends are often used in conjunction with other articulations. Pay attention to the phrasing of the following examples:

Position I:

Position II:

Position III:

Position IV:

Position VI:

This page has been left blank intentionally

Assignment:

Bendin' Tune

Chapter 8: Introduction to Position VII 8va, Sixteenth Note Syncopation with rests continued, and Counterpoint Reading in Positions I and II

In your career you will find the need to read passages an octave higher than written (8va) to be quite frequent. As the guitar sounds an octave lower than written, any time you are reading music in concert key (not specifically written for guitar) you must move passages up an octave to have them sound in their intended register. This would be the case when reading out of a fake book, off a lead sheet or piano score, or even when reading something composed by someone who isn't as familiar with a guitar's range as you are.

The easiest way to read a passage 8va would be to take a familiar position such as V and simply read it 12 frets higher (XVII).

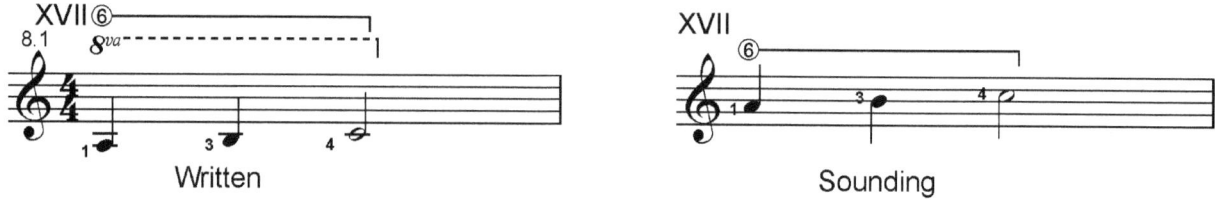

Try this strategy on the following exercise:

You will hopefully have had little trouble recognizing the pitches in this exercise as we are simply using the same recognition techniques as we have learned when becoming familiar with position V. However, you might have noticed the timbre of your guitar was rather thin, especially undesirable on the lower strings. I would suggest only reading this high on the neck when you are playing either passages that require you to be this high in your range or when you are in a situation where you have very minimal preparation time, and this would be the only way for you to perform with accuracy. Instead I would recommend doing much of your 8va reading in position VII.

Notes in Position VII 8va

The notes on the 6th string have not been included. These would get into the bass clef range and would not be necessary to read in the position. Notes below the low A would be increasingly unlikely as well. On the higher end you will find pitches included up to a high E on the 12th fret. Any passages that require higher pitches would best be player in a higher 8va position.

Interpret the following exercises in concert key and read them Position VII 8va:

C Major

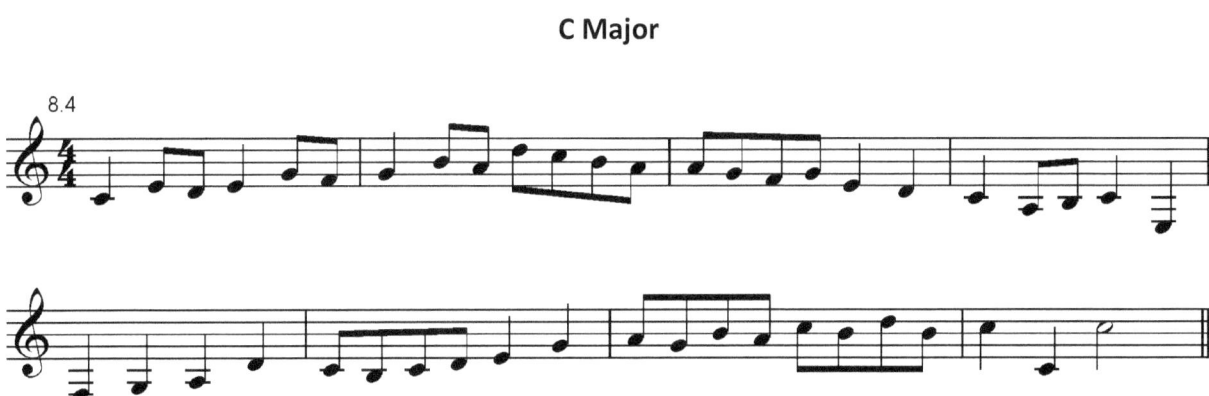

A Minor

F Major

D Minor

Bb Major

G Minor

G Major

E Minor

D Major

B Minor

8.28

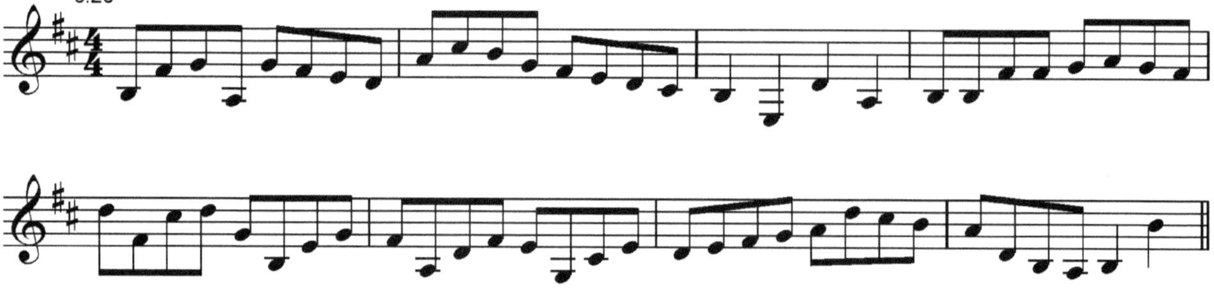

8.29

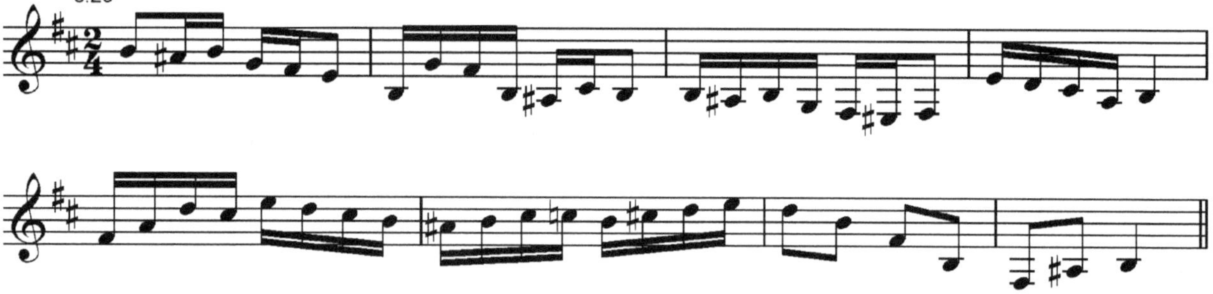

8.30

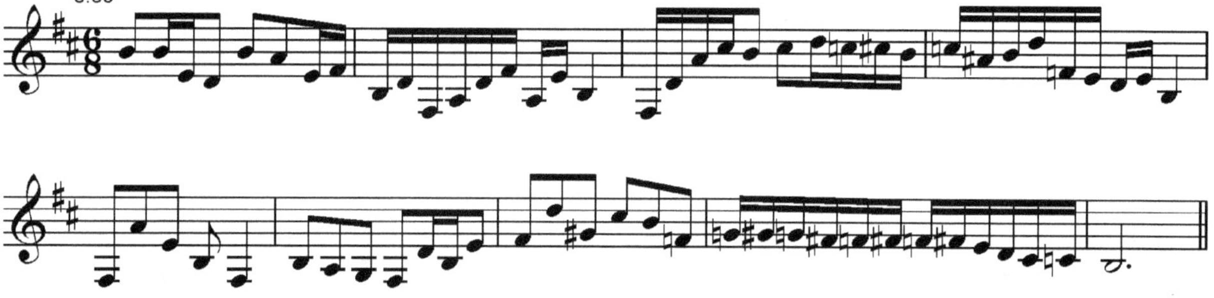

Sixteenth Note Rest Syncopation Continued

Play the rhythmic examples as many times as necessary before moving on to the melodic examples containing the same rhythms. Read in Position VII:

8.31

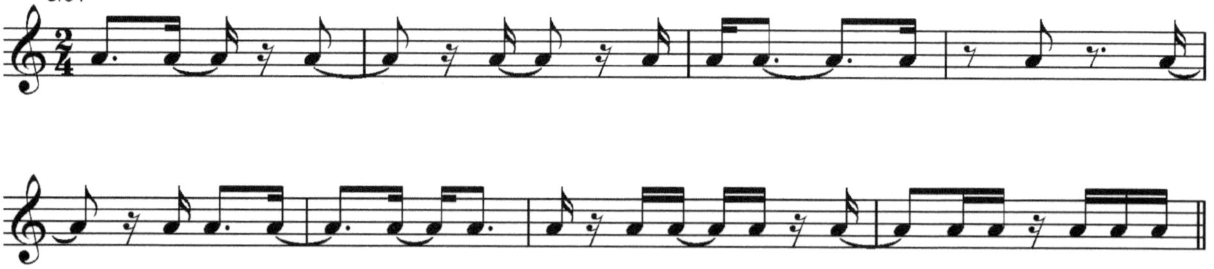

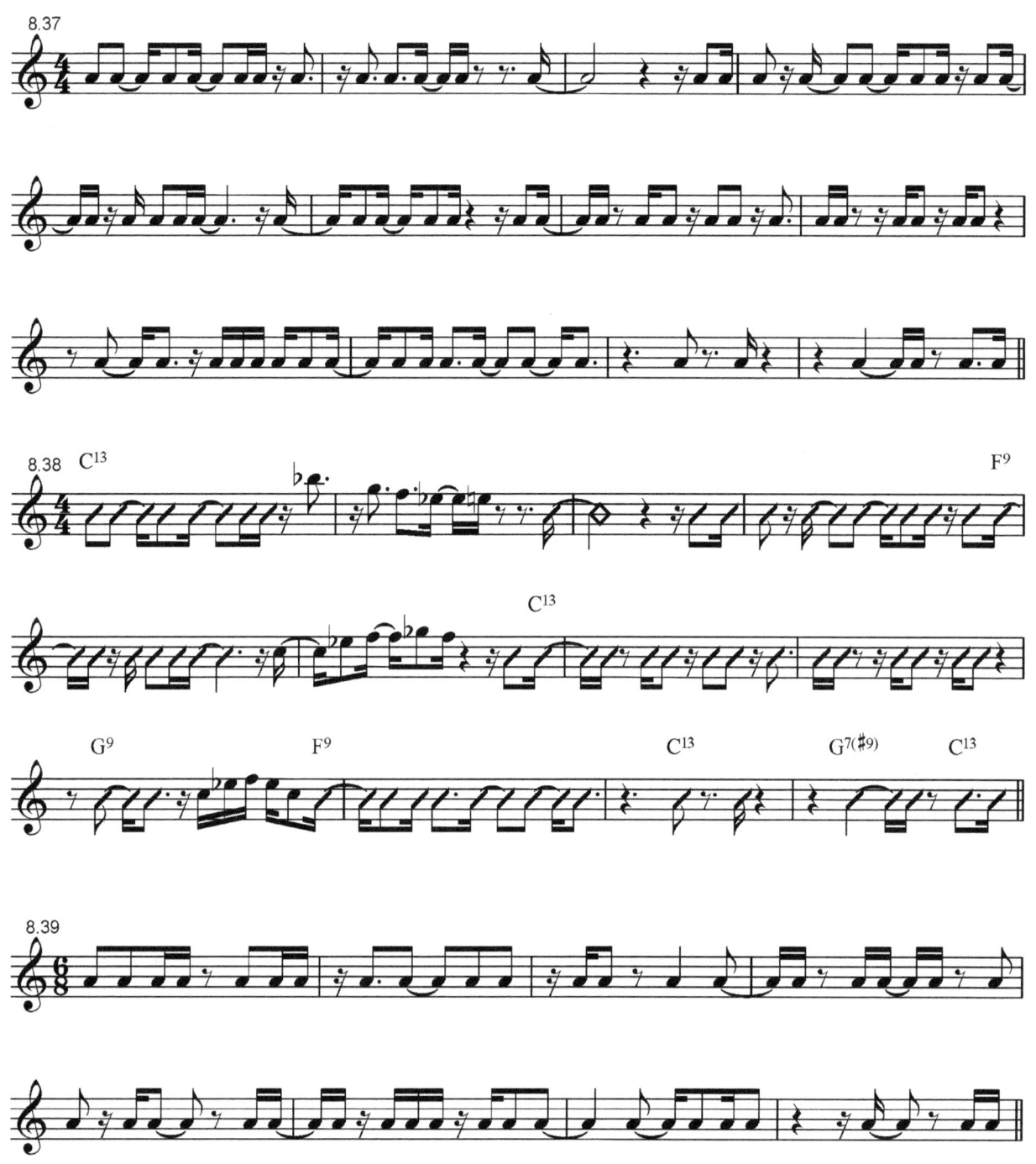

Counterpoint in Positions I and II Combined

Read the following examples in any combination of positions I and II needed to allow all notes to hold for their proper values:

Assignment:

Blowing Wind

Chapter 9: Position VII 8va Continued, Double Stop Bends, and Triple Stops in Positions I and V

Let us continue our study of Position VII 8va as you play the following exercises an octave higher than written:

Ab Major

F Minor

Db Major

Bb Minor

A Major

F# Minor

E Major

C# Minor

B Major

G# Minor

Double Stop Bends

A double stop bend occurs when two notes are played simultaneously and one (or both) notes are bent into. Double stop bends can bend into unisons or dyads, be bent and released, be pre-bent and released, or performed with any other inflections we have studied for single note bends.

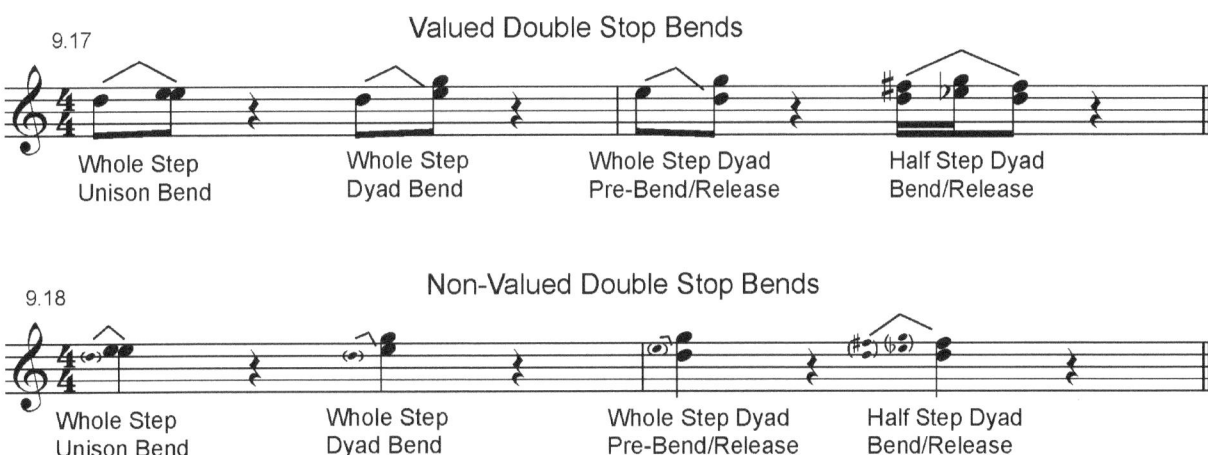

Try the following exercises in position V adhereing to all written bends and double stop bends:

9.22

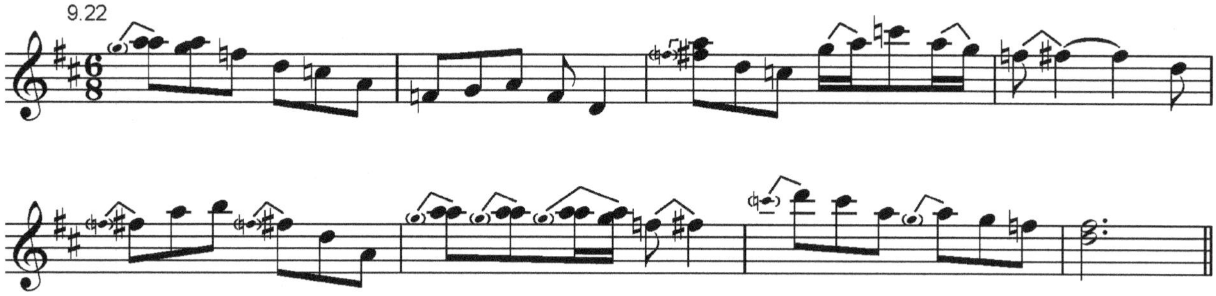

Try the following exercises in position II adhereing to all written bends and double stop bends:

9.23

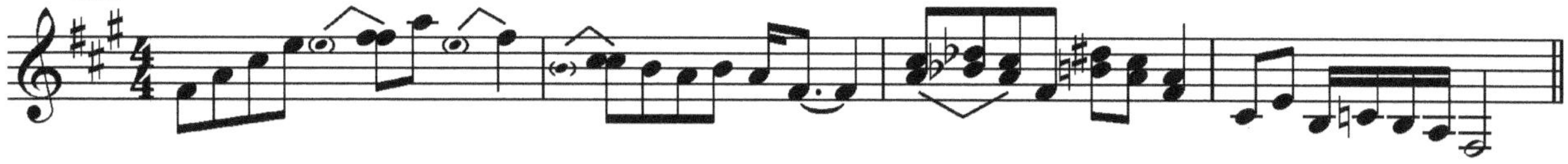

9.24

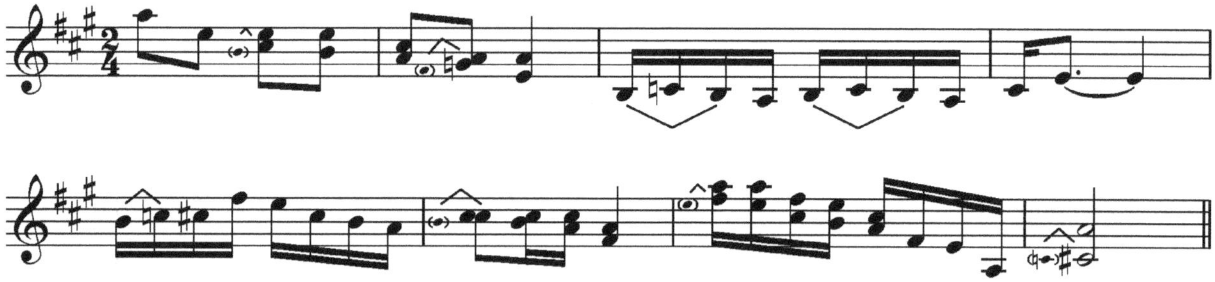

9.25

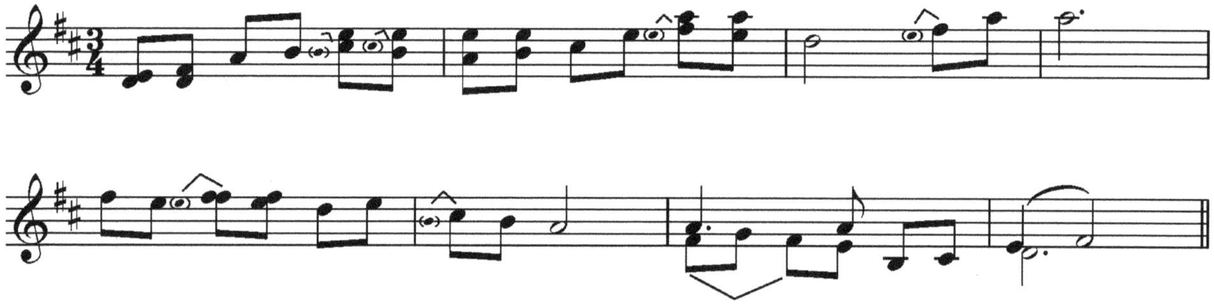

9.26

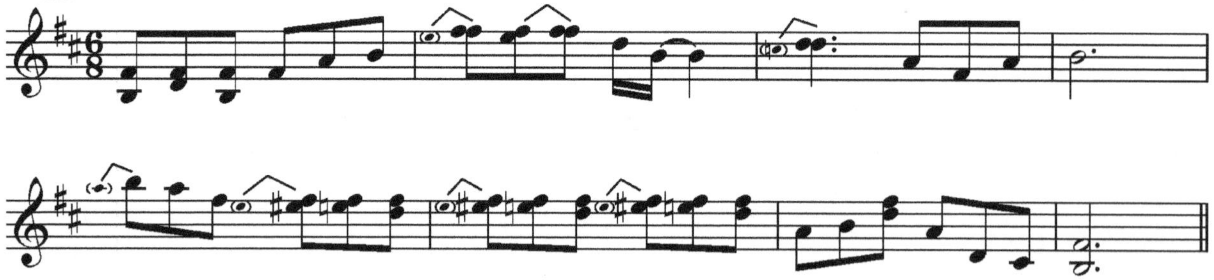

Triple Stop Reading

Triple stop reading expects you to recognize three separate pitches at once. Try to use your knowledge of intervallic distance recogniction and see triple stops as a combination of two interval sets. Read the following exercises in position I and use open strings as much as possible:

Read the following exercises in position V:

Assignment:

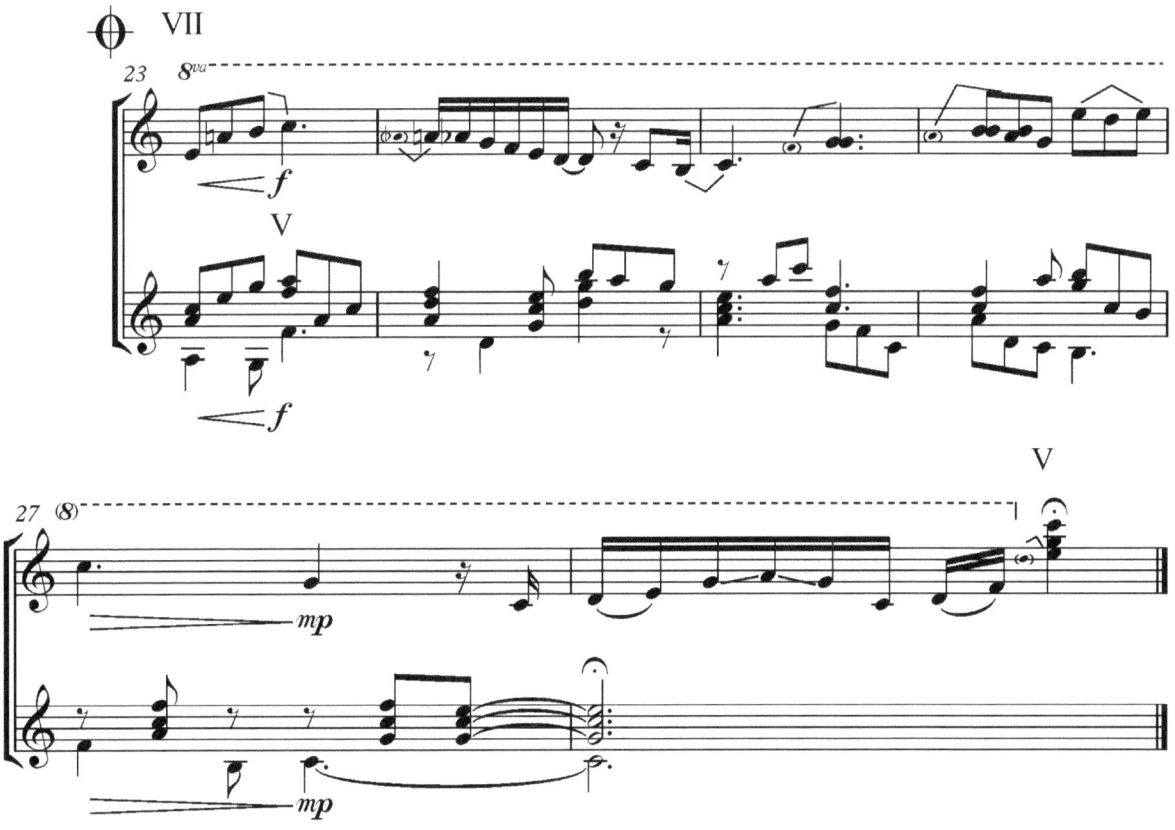

Chapter 10: Position VII 8va Continued, Positions V, VI and VII Combined, Triple Stop Reading in Positions I and II Combined, Articulation Review

Play the following exercises in position VII 8va:

Gb Major

Eb Minor

Cb Major

Ab Minor

F# Major

D# Minor

C# Major

A# Minor

Combining Positions V, VI and VII

The following exercises will feature phrases that modulate to different keys. Use the most convenient fingerings between the choices of Positions V, VI and VII:

10.18

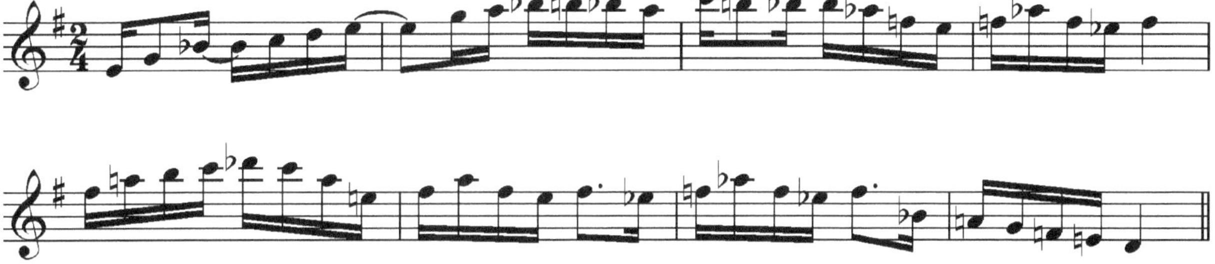

10.19

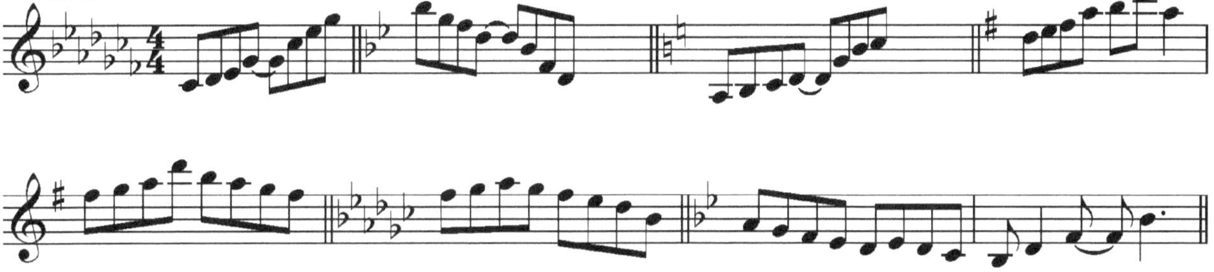

10.20

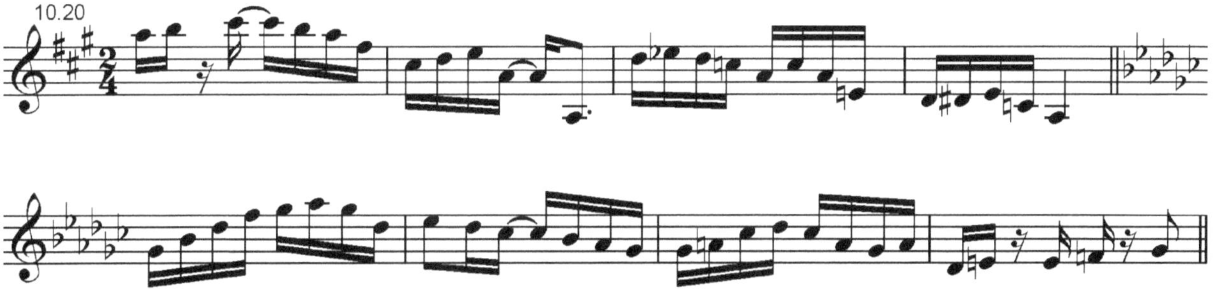

Triple Stop Reading in Positions I and II

Adjust between positions I and II as necessary in the following examples:

10.21

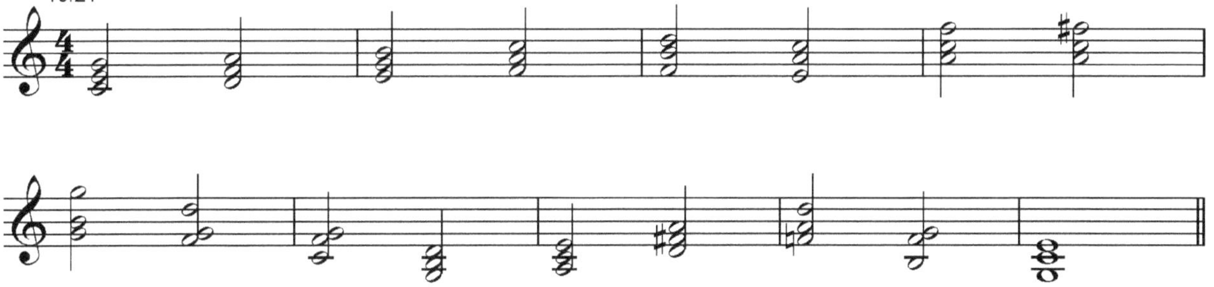

Reading Articulations: Palm Mutes, Let Rings, Bends, and Double Stop Bends

In the following examples, try to incorporate all articulations as marked:

Practice Charts:

Meddle

*All marked positions apply to notated passages only. Chord slashes may be played as desired.

The Pirate and the Insect

Funkenstein's Monster

About the Author

Ian Robbins graduated from USC with a Bachelor's and Master's degree in Studio/Jazz performance. He has had airplay on KJAZ 88.1FM and other national jazz stations as a member of the Bruce Escovitz Jazz Orchestra (BEJO). He recorded on BEJO's 2008 Album Invitation. Invitation spent several weeks in the top half of the Billboard Jazz charts. Ian recently recorded Guitar, Ukulele, and Mandolin tracks for a song used for a promotional video for the NBC TV Show *This Is Us* and for a movie trailer for *I Love You Berlin,* which starred Helen Mirren and Kira Knightly. Ian has performed with Landau Eugene Murphy Jr.- The winner of NBC's *America's Got Talent* Season 6. Ian has previously performed/recorded with Barry Manilow, Bonnie Raitt, Wynton Marsalis, Peter Erskine, Toni Tennille, Louis Bellson, Ndugu Chancellor, Stu Hamm, Kurt Elling, Ernie Watts, Marilyn McCoo, Alan Chang, Scott Henderson, and many others. Ian has also done session work for Grammy winning producer Bobby Watson and for Nickelodeon Studios. Recently Ian recorded for the JGAH project in Korea (arranged by Dr. Rachel Yoon), a Korean traditional music group that has performed live over 200 times along to Ian's prerecorded fusion guitar tracks.

Ian is currently on the faculty at Musician's Institute. As part of the Bachelor Degree Program he teaches Guitar Technique, Guitar Reading, Songwriting, Performance classes in Punk, Blues Rock and Fusion (the latter with former co/teacher Russell Ferrante), Ear Training, Private Lessons and Open Counseling. He also teaches the KPOP, Zawinul and Coffee House International LPWs. Ian has traveled, performed, and taught in Asia several times as part of MI's outreach program.

Ian Robbins is also the lead guitarist/singer/songwriter of original punk rock band Get Out™. Get Out™ has released 7 albums, which have sold on 6 continents and performed hundreds of shows. Get Out™'s YouTube channel currently has over 40,000 views (none of which were purchased). They have been endorsed by energy drink company Nitro 2 Go and have gotten airplay on various local stations. The band has performed on LA18 television and has shared the stage with such national acts as Voodoo Glow Skulls, Streetlight Manifesto, MXPX, and Suburban Legends. In January 2015, Get Out™ released *Epilogue* with the help of drummer Jeff Bowders (Paul Gilbert, Shakira). *Epilogue* is a 19 minute progressive punk rock epic currently being sold on iTunes and other online distributors. Get Out™ released their 7th album *We Were Here First* in 2019.

Ian is a member of Hip Hop/Electronica group Dancing Mischief, which has received airplay on KCRW FM.

Ian also plays guitar for Korean Grammy winning artist Ann One. Ann One has performed at KCON 2018, the Korean Society of Maryland's annual festival, on LA18's Halo Halo, and was featured on the pilot episode of the Asian American web series *Sessions at Studio 5A*.

Ian Robbins has published a book entitled *Beginning Guitar for the Songwriter* available online as both a print book and an ebook.

www.ingramcontent.com/pod-product-compliance
Lightning Source LLC
LaVergne TN
LVHW081529060526
838200LV00049B/2266